BUSY MOM'S GUIDE

to Parenting Young Children

Busy Mom's
GUIDE

to Parenting Young Children

PAUL C. REISSER, M.D.

Tyndale House Publishers, Inc.
Carol Stream, Illinois

THE OFFICIAL BOOK OF

THE
FOCUS ON
THE FAMILY
PHYSICIANS RESOURCE
COUNCIL, U.S.A.

Visit Tyndale online at www.tyndale.com.

Visit Focus on the Family at www.FocusOnTheFamily.com.

TYNDALE and Tyndale's quill logo are registered trademarks of Tyndale House
Publishers, Inc.

Focus on the Family and the accompanying logo and design are federally registered
trademarks of Focus on the Family, Colorado Springs, CO 80995.

Busy Mom's Guide to Parenting Young Children

Copyright © 2012 by Focus on the Family. All rights reserved.

Edited by Kara Conrad; produced with the assistance of The Livingstone Corporation.
Adapted from the *Complete Guide to Baby and Child Care*, ISBN 978-1-4143-1305-4. Copyright
© 2007 by Focus on the Family.

Cover photograph taken by Stephen Vosloo. Copyright © by Focus on the Family. All rights
reserved.

Designed by Jennifer Ghionzoli

Library of Congress Cataloging-in-Publication Data

Reisser, Paul C.
  Busy mom's guide to parenting young children / Paul C. Reisser.
      p. cm. — (Complete guides)
  Includes bibliographical references (p.   ) and index.
  ISBN 978-1-4143-6459-9 (sc)
1. Infants—Care. 2. Child care. 3. Child development. 4. Child rearing. I. Title.
  RJ61.R4164 2012
  649´.1—dc23   2011044279

Printed in the United States of America

18 17 16 15 14 13 12
7 6 5 4 3 2 1

CONTENTS

FIFTY YEARS AGO popular visions of the "world of tomorrow" included not only flying cars and routine trips to outer space, but also twenty- to thirty-hour workweeks and a bounty of leisure time for everyone by the end of the twentieth century.

Instead, more than a decade into the twenty-first century, we are dealing with exponential increases in the complexity our lives. We're working harder than ever to earn a living while juggling family responsibilities and a multitude of other commitments. Even when we're supposedly "off duty," there are always dozens of e-mails to wade through, cell phones sounding off at all hours, and social networking sites beckoning night and day. Furthermore, if we need information about anything, Google will be happy to summon more websites than we can possibly visit. Yet this overabundance of information sources doesn't always satisfy our need for wisdom and insight, especially when dealing with issues concerning some of the most important people in our lives: our children.

For more than three decades Focus on the Family has been a trusted resource for mothers and fathers as they have navigated the entire journey of parenting, from the first baby's cry in the delivery room to the release of their last young adult to (hopefully) responsible independence. Several years ago Focus on the Family's Physicians Resource Council prepared the *Complete Guide to Baby and Child Care,* and in 2007 a revised and expanded edition of this book was released. I had the privilege of serving as the primary author for both editions and can say without hesitation that the book was definitely *complete*, weighing in on virtually every topic related to parenting and the health of infants, children, and teens. At nine hundred pages, this was not a book to tuck into a handbag for a casual read over lunch.

Young children never fail to give parents plenty to think about (or lose sleep over), and busy schedules aren't always compatible with the task of sifting through the good and bad parenting advice on the Internet, or wading through the contents of a large book. We thus thought it would be helpful to distill the *Complete Guide*'s core concepts about parenting infants and young children into a smaller volume.

We have framed key ideas in the form of questions and answers, and have included a lot of practical advice, while trying to avoid a cookbook approach to parenting. Children are not built like cars or computers; they do not arrive with instruction manuals that guarantee that *B* will happen if you do *A*. Furthermore, what may work like a charm for your firstborn may prove to be an utter failure with child number two. Nevertheless, parenting is too important a task to approach without spending some time studying a basic road map and reviewing some trustworthy traveler's advisories.

This book is one in a series of Busy Mom's Guides, all of which are intended to provide help and hope for important concerns of family life. By the way, we would be very pleased if these guides would prove useful to some busy dads as well.

Paul C. Reisser, M.D.
November 2011

CHAPTER 1

PREPARING YOURSELF AND YOUR FAMILY

So you're getting ready to add a new member to your family. Congratulations! If this is your first child, you will probably have some apprehensions about the coming weeks—or, for that matter, about your baby's first days (and nights) at home. Will he get enough nourishment? How often should he be fed? Where should he sleep? Will *you* get any sleep? What if he starts crying—and won't stop? If there are other children at home, how will they respond to the new arrival?

Many of these questions may have already been addressed in a childbirth or parenting-preparation class. And if you have older children at home, you have already dealt with most of these concerns before and may not feel the need for any further "basic training." But just in case you didn't get all the bases covered, the second chapter will cover the ABCs of new baby care.

We begin, however, with a few important reminders about

taking care of yourself, your newborn, and the other important people in your life before and after the baby's birth.

How can my spouse and I make our marriage a priority after the baby arrives?

With all the excitement and changes that come with the role of parenting, whether for the first time or with a new addition, *it is extremely important that mother and father continuously reaffirm the importance of their own relationship.*

Mom, make sure your husband knows that he hasn't been relegated to the back burner of your affection and interest. Beware of total and absolute preoccupation with your new baby, as normal as that desire might seem to you. If you nurse, carry, rock, caress, and sleep with your baby twenty-four hours a day without offering some attention to your mate, before long your marriage may be a shadow of its former self.

Whenever possible, try to give some attention to your own needs and appearance, even if you're feeling exhausted. It's important that you establish a pattern of taking care of yourself even in these early days of motherhood, because from now on it will be tempting to neglect yourself when there are so many needs and tasks surrounding you. Taking care of yourself, even in small ways, can help you avoid baby-care burnout—not only now but also in the days and seasons to come.

Your husband and others will appreciate seeing you take steps to maintain your health and appearance as well.

Encourage your husband to pay lots of attention to your newborn. Remind him that he can cuddle, rock, and change the baby, and encourage him to roll up his sleeves and pitch in around the house. Don't forget to express appreciation for any help he offers.

Patterns you establish now in your marriage may well continue as your new baby and other children at home grow to maturity. Ultimately their sense of security will rise or fall with the visible evidence of stability, mutual respect, and ongoing love of their mother and father for one another. Overt demonstrations of affection not only fulfill deep and abiding needs between husband and wife, but they also provide a strong, daily reassurance for children that their world will remain intact.

The same can be said of time set aside by parents for quiet conversation with one another before (and after) the children have gone to bed. Make it a point to start or maintain the habit of asking each other a few key "checking in" questions, on a regular basis (at least weekly), and then listening carefully to the answers. These attentive conversations are an important safeguard against losing track of your spouse's thoughts and emotions, and they can help prevent an alarming realization months or years later: *I don't know my spouse anymore.*

Equally significant is a regular date night for Mom and Dad, which should be instituted as soon as possible and maintained even after the kids are grown and gone. These time-outs need not be expensive, but they may require some ongoing creativity, planning, and dedication. Dedication is necessary because child-care needs, pangs of guilt, and complicated calendars will conspire to prevent those dates from happening. But the romance, renewal, and vitality they generate are well worth the effort.

How can I prepare myself for life as a single parent?

Taking care of a new baby is a major project for a couple in a stable marriage. For a single parent—who usually, but not always, is the mother—the twenty-four-hour care of a newborn may seem overwhelming from the first day. But even without a committed partner, you *can* take care of your baby and do it well. The job will be less difficult if you have some help.

Hopefully, before the baby was born, you found a few people who would be willing members of your support team. These might be your parents, other relatives, friends, members of your church, or volunteers from a pregnancy resource center. By all means, don't hesitate to seek their help, especially during the early weeks when you are getting acquainted with your new baby. If your parents offer room, board, and child-care assistance, and you are on good terms with them, you would be wise to accept. Or if a helpful and mature family member or friend offers to stay with you for a while after the birth, give the idea careful consideration. (Obviously, you should avoid situations in which there is likely to be more conflict than help.)

Even after you have a few weeks or months of parenting under your belt, at some point you may need a brief time-out to walk around the block or advice on how to calm a colicky baby. But no one will know unless you ask. Many churches and pregnancy resource centers offer ongoing single-parent groups in which you can relax for a few hours on a regular basis, swap ideas, and talk with others who know firsthand the challenges you face. You might also make a short list of the names and numbers of trusted friends or relatives who have offered to be "SOS" resources—people you can call at any hour if you feel you've reached the end of your rope. Keep this list in a handy spot where you can find it at a moment's notice.

How can I prepare my other children for the arrival of the new baby?

Parents often worry about how the arrival of a new baby will affect other children in the family. Children's responses are as different as the children themselves. Some siblings will struggle with jealousy for a while; others will welcome the new baby excitedly, eager to be "big sister" or "big brother." But most children, especially if they are younger than age six or seven, will experience a range of emotions: happiness, jealousy, possessiveness toward the baby, protectiveness, fear of being forgotten by the parents, fear that there won't be enough love in the family to go around.

While parents can't prevent the onset of these emotions, they can do much to prepare children for an additional person in the family.

- Talk about the baby's coming well in advance.

- Include your other children in discussions about the baby.

- Be careful about how much the arrangements for the baby will impinge on other children's space in the house and schedule.

- Make plans for other relatives to pay attention to the other children.

- Pay attention to signs of jealousy or other forms of upset.

- Direct visitors' attention to the other children.

How should I choose a health-care provider for my baby?

Your options for the baby's health-care provider may include a pediatrician, who has a medical degree and at least three years of residency training in the care of infants, children, and adolescents. Pediatricians are considered primary-care physicians—that is, they serve as the point of entry into the health-care system. They provide routine checkups and manage the vast majority of illnesses and other children's health problems. A neonatologist specializes in the care of premature infants and sick newborns, usually in an intensive-care unit.

Family practitioners (whether holding M.D. or D.O. degrees) care for all age-groups, including infants and children. Family practitioners may request consultation from pediatricians or subspecialists when dealing with more difficult cases.

Pediatricians and family physicians may also employ nurse practitioners and physician assistants, who are trained to provide basic services in an office setting. They are often more readily accessible, particularly for same-day appointments, and may be able to spend more time answering questions and working through common problems.

Your insurance company, local hospital, or—even better—your family doctor, family members, or friends may be good sources of physician recommendations. Once you've narrowed your list, you might consider setting a brief meet-the-doctor session with a few health-care providers at the top of the list. That will give you an opportunity to judge the friendliness and helpfulness of the office staff, meet the physician, and check payment policies.

What basic clothing and equipment should I invest in before bringing my baby home?

Clothing. Your baby's wardrobe, commonly referred to as a layette, should include several lightweight receiving blankets, sleeper sets, light tops, undershirts, socks, sweaters, hats or bonnets, and one or two sets of baby washcloths and towels.

Consider safety issues when buying clothes—snaps are safer than buttons that could be pulled off and swallowed; material should be flame-retardant.

Diapers. Whether you choose disposable for their convenience or cloth for their lower cost over time, be sure to stock up before baby's arrival.

Furniture. A cradle or bassinet offers convenience for the newborn's parents; a crib will serve your baby for the first two or three years. Be sure the slats in a crib are no wider than two and three-eighths inches (six centimeters) apart. A changing table provides a convenient place for diaper duties. Look for one with a two-inch guardrail around its edge and a safety strap to help you secure the baby. (These, however, should never be considered a substitute to a caregiver's undivided attention when your infant is on the changing table.)

Car seat. *Every* infant, toddler, and young child must be properly secured into an appropriate car seat every time she rides in a car. In fact, hospitals will not even allow parents to leave their facility with their newborns if they don't have one. The car seat for a newborn should be either an infant-only or convertible model manufactured within the last ten years. An infant-only carrier will double as a carrier; a convertible seat can be reconfigured to face forward when the baby reaches her first birthday *and* weighs twenty pounds (just over nine kilograms).

Because the newborn has no head control, she must face backward in the car to prevent dangerous, rapid forward movement of the head during sudden stops. To help reduce the chance of injury further:

- Don't use a seat that is the wrong size for the infant or child.

- Don't use an outdated car seat.

- Be sure to secure the seat properly in the vehicle and the child correctly in the seat. (Local law-enforcement agencies, fire stations, and health departments will often conduct free safety checks.)

- Learn how to adjust the shoulder harnesses correctly.

- Do not put a rear-facing car seat in front of an air bag.

Why should I consider breastfeeding?
Human milk is uniquely suited to human babies. It is not only nutritionally complete and properly balanced, but it is also constantly changing to meet the needs of a growing infant. The fat

content of breast milk increases as a feeding progresses, creating a sense of satisfied fullness that tends to prevent overeating. Indeed, a number of studies indicate that being breastfed as an infant may offer modest protection against becoming overweight and developing diabetes later in life.

Furthermore, the fat and cholesterol content of breast milk is higher in the early months, when these compounds are most needed in a baby's rapidly growing brain and nervous system. The primary proteins in all forms of milk are whey and casein, but in human milk, whey, which is easier to absorb, predominates. Compared to cow's milk, the carbohydrate component of breast milk contains a higher percentage of lactose, which appears to play an important role in both brain development and calcium absorption.

Vitamins and minerals are adequately supplied in mother's milk. Vitamins and minerals (including trace elements such as copper and zinc) are present in the right amounts, and iron is present in breast milk in a form that is easier for the baby to absorb than that found in any other type of milk. As a result, no supplements are needed for the normal breastfed infant—with one exception.

Breast milk alone does not contain enough vitamin D to ensure proper bone development. This vitamin is manufactured in the skin in response to exposure to sunlight. But since direct exposure to sunlight can pose potential hazards to the sensitive skin of a young infant (see page 76), professional organizations such as the American Academy of Pediatrics (AAP) recommend routine use of sunscreen.

In order to provide adequate vitamin D without risking sun damage to an infant's skin, the AAP recommends that an infant who is fed only breast milk also receive 400 international units (IU) of vitamin D every day by dropper, beginning in the first few days after birth. This amount of vitamin D should also be given to formula-fed infants who are taking less than 34 ounces (about 1000 cc, a little more than a quart) per day. Infant formula contains vitamin D, but a baby needs to consume 34 ounces or more per day to receive an adequate amount of this vitamin.[1]

Breast milk is absorbed extremely efficiently, with little undigested material passing into stool. Experienced diaper changers are well aware that formula-fed infants tend to have smellier stools, a by-product of the nutritional odds and ends (especially certain fats and proteins) that are not thoroughly absorbed on their trip through the bowel.

From day one, breast milk contains antibodies that help protect babies from infections. The first product of the breast after birth, known as colostrum, is particularly rich in antibodies known as immunoglobulin A, which help protect the lining of the intestine from microscopic invaders. As the mother comes in contact with new viruses and bacteria, her immune system generates the appropriate microbe-fighting antibodies and passes them on to her baby, thus reducing—but by no means eliminating—the newborn's risk of becoming infected. This is particularly important in the first several months, when the newborn's immune system is less effective at mounting a defense against microscopic invaders.

While formula manufacturers have labored mightily to duplicate the nutritional mixture of breast milk, they cannot hope to supply any of these complex immune factors. Current research has provided strong evidence that feeding infants with human milk decreases the incidence (number of cases) and severity of a wide range of infectious diseases, including otitis media (middle ear infections), diarrhea, respiratory infections, bacterial meningitis, and urinary tract (bladder and kidney) infections.[2]

Breastfeeding may reduce the risk of a variety of serious health problems. Some research indicates a reduced risk of sudden infant death syndrome (SIDS) among breastfed infants. Older children and adults who were breastfed as infants may be less likely to develop diabetes, obesity, elevated cholesterol levels, asthma, and certain types of cancer (specifically leukemia, lymphoma, and Hodgkin's disease).[3]

Breast milk is free. It is clean, fresh, warm, and ready to feed, anytime and virtually anyplace. It does not need to be purchased, stored (although it can be expressed into bottles and frozen for later use), mixed, or heated.

Breastfeeding offers several health benefits for Mom. Stimulation of a mother's nipples by a nursing infant releases a hormone called oxytocin, which helps her uterus to contract toward what will become its nonpregnant size. The hormonal response to nursing also postpones the onset of ovulation and the menstrual cycle, providing a natural—although not foolproof—spacing of children. Nursing mothers also tend to reach their prepregnancy weight more quickly. In addition, some research indicates that breastfeeding may reduce a woman's chance of developing breast and ovarian cancer, osteoporosis, and hip fractures later in life.

Breastfeeding lends itself to a sense of closeness, intimacy, and mutual satisfaction. The skin-to-skin contact, the increased sensory input for the baby, and the mother's satisfaction in being able to provide her child's most basic needs can help establish strong bonds between them.

Are there any reasons *not* to breastfeed?

There are a few medical situations in which breastfeeding poses a risk for the baby. HIV, the virus responsible for AIDS, can be transmitted from an infected mother to a noninfected infant through nursing, and thus a woman infected with HIV should not breastfeed her infant. A mother with active, untreated tuberculosis should not nurse her baby. Hepatitis C is not transmitted through breast milk, but it is spread through infected blood. A nursing mother with hepatitis C should temporarily stop nursing if her nipples or the area surrounding them become cracked or bleed.

Obviously, breastfeeding may be extremely difficult or even unsafe for both mother and child if the mother has a serious illness. Furthermore, virtually all medications show up to some degree in breast milk, and some are potentially harmful for infants. If a new mother needs to take one or more drugs that are necessary to preserve her life and health but are unsafe for a baby (for example, cancer chemotherapy), formula feeding should be used. Careful consultation with both mother's and baby's physicians is in order when making this decision.

Previous breast surgery may affect a mother's ability to nurse. A biopsy or local lump removal in the past normally will not cause difficulty. Even after a mastectomy, it is possible to feed a baby adequately using the remaining breast. Breast-reduction surgery, however, may result in an inadequate milk supply if the majority of milk-producing tissue has been removed. Previous breast-enhancement/implant surgery should not cause a problem for nursing unless the ducts that carry milk to the nipple were cut during the procedure.

Infants born with phenylketonuria (PKU) or galactosemia, rare metabolic disorders that are detected by routine screening tests after birth, must be fed special formulas to prevent a variety of serious consequences.

Congenital problems such as a cleft lip or palate, heart disease, and Down syndrome can create special challenges for nursing. However, the benefits of mother's milk for these infants are usually well worth the extra effort needed to provide it for them, even if they cannot obtain milk directly from the breast. A team effort (involving parents, physicians, and a lactation consultant) will be necessary in these situations.

A number of nonmedical concerns might cause a woman to be reluctant to breastfeed or to consider abandoning it too quickly. These are worth some review and reflection.

A previous bad experience. Perhaps you have an older child who wouldn't, couldn't, or didn't want to nurse. After days of frustration, tears, and sore nipples, you may have finally given her a bottle.

If you had difficulty nursing a baby in the past, remember that each newborn is different. There is no rule that says history must repeat itself, and there are, in fact, very few women who simply are unable to supply enough milk to sustain their offspring.

Physical problems. You may wonder if your breasts are too small or too big to nurse, or if flat, dimpled, or inverted nipples will prevent you from doing so.

Actually, your milk is supplied by mammary (milk-producing) glands, whose function is not related to breast size. In response to large amounts of hormones circulating during pregnancy—especially prolactin (literally, "for milk"), estrogen, progesterone, and human placental lactogen (which, as its name indicates, is secreted by the placenta)—the mammary glands enlarge, mature, and become capable of producing milk. However, the actual process of creating milk is held in check during pregnancy by these same elevated hormone levels. When your baby is born and the placenta delivered, the abrupt loss of placental hormones allows milk production to begin in earnest—whether you plan to nurse or not. This interplay between multiple hormones and structures within the body is intricately designed, and you can assume that it will function as intended.

Nipples may vary in shape, and some may be easier for infants to grasp and suck than others. Those that clearly protrude may look like better nursing candidates than those that are flat, dimpled, or inverted. What matters most, however, is what happens when the infant attempts to latch on and suck. To get a preview, gently squeeze *behind* the nipple using thumb and index finger.

If your nipple clearly extends outward in response to this squeeze, your baby should have little difficulty. If your nipple flattens or inverts further, however, you may have tiny adhesions under the skin that are preventing it from extending outward. Normally, changes in the breast related to pregnancy will help correct this problem. However, if the squeeze test is still yielding a flat or inverted nipple by the last trimester of pregnancy, a breast shield may help. This is a simple plastic device, worn inside the bra, that exerts constant gentle pressure on the areola and gradually helps the nipple protrude. If help is needed after birth, a shield can be worn between feedings.

Don't try to toughen up your nipples by pulling or rubbing them before or during pregnancy. Not only will this fail to prevent any soreness during nursing, but it might stimulate the release of hormones that can cause the uterus to contract or even begin labor prematurely. (Nursing an older child may also cause premature contractions. If this happens, the child must be weaned immediately.)

Lifestyle issues. Perhaps you're thinking, *I don't want to be the only one who can feed the baby. I've seen women whose babies are like appendages stuck permanently on their chests. They have no life—they can't go anywhere or do anything without their baby.*

Breastfeeding does take more of Mom's time, but it need not be a ball-and-chain experience. After nursing has become a well-established routine, milk can be expressed into a bottle and stored for Dad, grandparents, or babysitters to use at a later date. And if you need to get away for a long evening or even overnight, it won't harm your baby to have a formula feeding or two if you don't have enough of your own milk in the freezer. Don't forget that nursing means being free from the expense and hassle of buying formula; preparing it; and dealing with nipples, bottles, bottle liners, and other items.

Returning to work. "I need to return to my job in two months, and I don't see how I can spend eight or ten hours in the office at the same time I'm trying to nurse."

In 2010, Congress passed legislation that requires employers to provide reasonable break time and private spaces for women to express milk for their nursing children for up to one year after their babies' birth. Even one or two months of nursing are worth doing, and believe it or not, with some planning, creativity, and assistance on the home front, it is possible for a breastfeeding mother to return to work. The adjustments will vary considerably with the age of the baby, the location of the job, and the hours involved.

CHAPTER 2

●●● THE FIRST THREE MONTHS

IF YOU ARE bringing home a new baby for the very first time, you have probably been wondering what your life will be like on a day-to-day basis. Perhaps you have envisioned your new parenthood as a tranquil scene from a greeting card or a TV commercial: a contented mother and father sitting by the fireside, smiling softly at the tiny cherub who sweetly coos her love in return. Or you may have heard tales of misery from family or friends who have complained about sleepless nights, relentless fatigue, and no life at all away from the seven-pound tyrant who demands attention every moment. If you already have children, you know that neither of these visions accurately encompasses the breadth and depth of caring for a newborn.

Because every baby, parent, and family situation is unique, cookbook approaches to baby care, with step-by-step directions for every situation, are unrealistic. Instead, as we look at the elements of your new baby's daily routine, we will outline some basic facts and principles that you can then adapt and fine-tune to your family's unique circumstances.

Above all, try your best to relax and trust that you and your baby will in fact eventually settle in (and settle down) together.

What should I expect from my baby during these first few months?

Nursing, sleeping, and crying may dominate a newborn's time during the first several weeks; however, your baby will also be quietly alert about 10 percent of the time early on. As the weeks pass, you will begin to notice that your baby is spending more time in calm and active alertness, during which you will see several wonderful developments in a variety of areas:

Vision. During the first few weeks, a baby focuses best on objects eight to fifteen inches (about 20 to 40 cm) from her face. You may find her staring intently at the fist at the end of her outstretched arm, which happens to be in her focusing range. She will prefer to study plain, high-contrast, black-and-white images such as stripes, checks, or spirals, or a simple drawing of a face. She may gaze intently into a small, unbreakable mirror attached to the inside of her crib. But her favorite subject to scrutinize will be the face of another person, about a foot away from hers. She will not respond directly to a smile for a few weeks, but a lot of smiles are what she should see.

Your baby will be able to follow an object with her eyes only momentarily at first. You can give her some practice at this ability by moving your face or a brightly colored object slowly from side to side across her field of vision. Around two months of age, she will be able to coordinate her eye movements to stay locked on an interesting visual target that passes through a semicircle in front of her. She will also be interested in more complex shapes and patterns and will be able to hold her head steady enough to fixate on simple, high-contrast objects hung from a mobile over her crib. By three months of age, her distant vision will be increased to the point that she will recognize you halfway across a room.

Responses to color also develop over the first several weeks. At first she will pay attention to objects with bright, strongly contrasting colors. Ironically, the soft colors that are so often used in decorating a baby's room won't be particularly interesting to her at first. It will take a few months before her color vision has matured enough to distinguish a full palette and varieties of shades.

From time to time, all babies will briefly cross their eyes as they develop their tracking skills. But if she frequently appears to have crossed eyes at the age of three months or later, she should be checked as soon as possible by her physician and an ophthalmologist. Why is this important? If the position of her eyes is constantly presenting two images instead of one to her brain, she will shut down the information arriving from one eye or the other, resulting in amblyopia, or lazy eye.

Hearing. Newborns vary in their sensitivity to sounds. Some infants seem capable of sleeping through a violent thunderstorm, while others appear to startle when a cat crosses the street a block away. If a young infant is placed in a very noisy environment, he may appear to "shut down," markedly reducing his activity level. This is a protective mechanism, an internal withdrawal from a situation that is overloading him. While you don't need to maintain a hushed silence around your newborn, you should try to keep the noise level around him at a comfortable level—no more than, for example, the intensity of pleasant conversation between two or three people. If you want to go to a ball game or a concert (or even a church service) where the sound is likely to be pumped up, leave the baby at home.

Within a few weeks, he will appear to pay attention to certain sounds, especially the voices of those who regularly care for him. By two months of age, he may begin to shift his eyes and head toward your voice. He may also show some movements and expressions indicating that he recognizes this familiar and comforting sound. As he continues toward three months of age, you will notice him starting to turn toward other interesting sounds, such as a tinkling bell. If the sound is repeated over and over, however, he will tune it out and stop responding to it.

Smell. A very young baby is capable of responding to a variety of smells and can distinguish the smell of his mother's breast from those of other nursing mothers by the end of the first week of life.

Touch. All of us are strongly affected by touch, but a baby is particularly sensitive. She will startle in response to scratchy surfaces, rough handling, or sudden temperature changes—especially when her skin makes contact with something cold. Cuddling, caressing, and stroking may help calm a crying episode, but these shouldn't be used merely to stop tears. Touch is an important expression of love and will nourish her emotions before she can understand any words. It should be as routine a part of her day as her feedings.

These developments set the stage for your baby's first true socializing, which will probably begin just as you are starting to wonder whether all the nursing and diapers and nonstop caregiving are worth it. You may first notice a brief flicker of a grin after a feeding. Was that a smile or a gas pain? Maybe it was both or maybe neither, but it felt like a puff of fresh air on a hot day. Suddenly—at about the age of four to six weeks—it will be unmistakable: You will lock eyes with your baby, and a big grin will flash across her face. It will be an unforgettable moment, and the next time she smiles will be equally rewarding because you'll know that this milestone was for real.

Over the next month, you will catch smiles in response to

your own grinning, cooing, talking, or singing to your baby. You may notice special enthusiastic body movements in response to familiar voices and the turning of eyes and head to seek them out. Even more pleasant are your first "conversations." At about two months, your baby will begin to coo, often in response to your speaking to her in soft, soothing tones. At this age, she will not understand the words you speak, but the tone of your voice will communicate volumes.

Growth and movement. Babies lose and then regain several ounces (about a tenth of their birth weight) during the first ten days after birth. From then on, you can anticipate a weight gain of about two-thirds to one ounce per day, or one to two pounds per month (20 to 30 grams per day, or 450 to 900 grams per month). Your baby will add between one and one and a half inches (or about 2.5 to 4 cm) in height each month as well. These amounts will vary, of course, depending on your baby's feeding patterns and on genetics, which will affect whether this growing body will ultimately resemble a ballerina or a fullback. During each medical checkup, your baby's height, weight, and head circumference will be measured and then plotted on a growth chart. Tracking your baby's growth will be an important tool for her health-care provider to confirm how well she is doing.

During the first three months, you will see dramatic changes in your baby's movement patterns. At birth her arms and legs flail and jerk, her chin may twitch, and her hands may tremble. Many of her movements are reflexes, such as rooting, sucking, and grasping. In addition, you may see her do a "fencing" maneuver known as the tonic neck reflex: If her head is turned in one direction, you may see the arm on that side straighten and the other arm flex, as if she were about to enter a sword fight. In addition, if you gently hold her body upright, supporting her head, and then lower her gently until her feet touch a firm surface, she will begin stepping motions. This has nothing to do with how soon she will begin walking, and this so-called stepping reflex will be gone by the age of two months. However, she will kick her legs quite vigorously when awake and active while lying on her back or stomach.

Hand and arm movements will gradually become less jerky and almost appear purposeful. Between two and three months, she will begin to spend more time with her hands open rather than clenched and will bring them toward her mouth or in front of her face, where she may appear to study them. She still won't have the coordination to reach directly for something that interests her, although she will tightly grasp a small object placed in her hand. In fact, you may have to help her let it go.

At two months she will have developed enough control of her neck muscles to hold her head in one position while lying on her back. When lying on her stomach, she will be able to raise her head briefly, just long enough to turn it from one side to another. But her head control overall will not be secure until three to four months of age, so you must support her head whenever you hold or carry her.

What are the breastfeeding basics?

Whenever you begin, you and your baby should be able to find a position that not only is comfortable but also allows him to latch on to the breast properly. This occurs when his mouth closes over the areola (the dark area surrounding the nipple) and forms a seal with his gums. When properly attached, a baby should grasp the entire areola and not just the nipple itself. His tongue should be positioned against the underside of the nipple, and then with wavelike motions compress it, emptying the milk-containing ducts just below the areola.

If he repeatedly clamps down on the nipple only and not the areola, you will probably develop some major pain and cracking in the nipple before long—and have a frustrated baby as well because he won't get much milk this way. Some babies at first seem more interested in licking or nibbling than in grasping the breast properly. While it is a good idea in general to avoid bottle feedings during the first several days unless absolutely necessary, it is particularly important that these "lick and chew" newborns stay away from formula and pacifiers until they catch on to latching on.

If you nurse immediately after delivery, it will usually be easiest to lie on your side with the baby's entire body facing you, stomach to stomach. This position will also be very useful in the days following a cesarean delivery, in order to prevent the weight of the baby from pressing on your sore abdomen. In this position you will need to lift your breast with the opposite hand to move the areola next to his mouth.

More common is the *sitting cuddle position*, in which the infant's head is cradled in the bend of your elbow with your forearm supporting his back and your hand holding his bottom or upper leg. An alternative sitting position, called the *football hold*, places your baby's body at your side, supported by your arm with your hand holding his head. This position can be helpful if you have had a cesarean birth, since it minimizes pressure on your incision site, and it is also useful for mothers of twins who wish to nurse both babies simultaneously. The football hold can also help babies who are having a harder time getting attached properly, since they face the breast straight on without having to turn their heads.

Once you are positioned comfortably, gently lift your breast and stroke your baby's cheek or lower lip with your nipple. This will provoke his rooting reflex. When his mouth opens wide, gently pull him to you so that your areola enters his mouth. You will need to make this move relatively quickly before his mouth closes. Be sure not to meet him halfway by leaning forward, or else you will have a very sore back before long. It helps to compress your breast slightly between thumb and palm or between two fingers in a scissorlike position, using your free hand, but stay a couple of inches behind the areola when you do so.

When your baby begins sucking, nerve endings in the nipple send a message to the pituitary gland at the base of your brain. The pituitary in turn secretes the hormone prolactin, which stimulates more milk production, and oxytocin, which causes tiny muscles that surround the milk ducts to squeeze milk toward the areola. This event is called the let-down reflex, which you will probably feel as a change of pressure or, less commonly, as a tingling within the breasts. Some women, however, can't feel the let-down reflex at all. Once your milk has come in, you may notice anything from a slow drip of milk to a full-blown spray during let-down. Many women will experience let-down not only in response to their baby's sucking but also when their baby—or someone else's— begins to cry. During the first days after delivery, you will also feel contractions of the uterus in response to the oxytocin released by the pituitary gland. While these might be uncomfortable, they are carrying out the important function of reducing the size of your uterus.

The let-down reflex may be inhibited by certain drugs, as well as by smoking. Let-down also may not function as well if you are upset or tense. It is therefore important that your nursing times be as relaxed and calm as possible. You might consider setting up a comfortable "nursing corner" at home, where your favorite chair (very often a rocker) and a table with soft light, a few key supplies, soft music, and even something to read are within easy reach. A small stash of healthy snack food and some water or juice would be an appropriate addition as well. Not only is it important that mothers remain well hydrated while nursing, but they often experience considerable thirst during let-down.

Remember that for the first three or four days you will be producing colostrum, the yellowish, high-protein liquid full of antibodies and white blood cells. With rare exception, this is all your baby will need, since he was born with extra fluid in his system that compensates for the relatively low fluid volume of colostrum. When your milk supply begins to arrive, you will notice some increased fullness, warmth, and probably tenderness. During this process, your breasts are said to be engorged, and they may actually swell so much that your baby will have trouble latching on to them. Should this occur, you can gently express some milk from each breast, softening it so your baby can grasp more easily. To express milk, grasp the edge of the areola between thumb and fingers and then repeatedly squeeze while pushing gently toward your chest. (A warm compress or hot shower may be needed to get the milk flowing.)

What are some common infant nursing patterns?

Each baby has a unique style of nursing, and yours may mesh easily with your milk supply and lifestyle or may require that you make some adjustments. Some infants get right down to business, sucking vigorously and efficiently without much hesitation. These "barracudas" contrast sharply with the "gourmet" nursers, who take their sweet time, playing with the nipple at first, sampling their meal, and then eventually getting started. Some babies vary the gourmet approach by resting every few minutes, as if savoring their feeding, or even falling asleep one or more times during the nursing session. The "suck and snooze" types may exasperate a mother who feels that she doesn't have all day to nurse. While it's all right to provide a little mild stimulation (such as undressing her) to get Sleepy back on task and complete her feeding, some downsizing of your expectations for the day's activities may be necessary to prevent ongoing frustration.

Newborns also vary in the frequency with which they need to nurse. A typical span between feedings will be two to three hours, or eight to twelve times per day, but during the first days after birth, the interval may be longer, with only six to eight feedings in a twenty-four-hour period. The baby will feed more often than usual during growth spurts. The time involved in a feeding will also vary, but a typical feeding will take ten to fifteen minutes per breast.

Don't worry if your baby doesn't seem terribly interested in frequent nursing during the first few days. That will change, often just after you bring her home. The early phase of sleepiness that occurs as she adjusts to the outside world will usually give way to more active crying and nursing—sometimes every few hours—after the first week. Some parents are aghast when this happens. The mellow baby they enjoyed in the hospital suddenly seems wired and insatiable just a few days later. Don't panic. Instead, look at this as a time to hone your nursing skills with a very willing partner.

The newborn baby will announce her desire for milk every two to four hours in a number of ways. Some of these are subtle—looking alert, fidgeting a little, moving her mouth or tongue—and some more overt, such as sucking on her hand or rooting toward your breast (or the chest of whoever is holding her). Insistent crying is a *late* sign of hunger, and there's no point in waiting for her to reach that level of discomfort before offering the breast. (Indeed, nursing is likely to proceed more smoothly if she is calm rather than agitated.) If she is showing signs of hunger, it is appropriate to tend to her promptly, change her if necessary, and then settle in for a feeding.

For five to ten minutes you will notice her swallowing after every few sucks, and then she will shift to a more relaxed mode or even seem to lose interest. She can then be burped, either by lifting her and placing her head over your shoulder, or by sitting her up with your hand under her jaw and gently patting her on the back. You can also place her facedown across your lap, with head supported and chest a little higher than abdomen, and gently pat her back.

Once she burps, she may show interest in the other breast. (If she doesn't burp and yet appears comfortable, you can still proceed with the feeding.) Since the first side may be more completely emptied during the feeding, it is wise to alternate the breast from which she starts. (A small pin or clip that you move from one side of your nursing bra to the other can help remind you where to begin next time.)

Relatively frequent nursing is typical after the first days of life, and it will help stimulate your milk production and let-down reflex. A newborn who seems to be very content with infrequent feedings (more than four hours apart) should probably be checked by your physician to confirm that her activity level is satisfactory. She may in fact need to be awakened to feed every three hours to ensure adequate weight gain during the first two or three weeks.

When I'm nursing, how do I know my baby is getting enough nourishment?

During the first few days after birth, this concern often prods new mothers toward bottle-feeding, where they have the security of seeing exactly how much the baby is consuming. Remember that the quantity of milk you produce during a feeding will start with as little as half an ounce (15 ml) of colostrum during the first day or two and increase to an ounce (30 ml) as the milk supply arrives by the fourth or fifth day. After the first week, your milk output will range from two to six ounces (about 60 to 180 ml) per feeding. Obviously, there is no direct way for you to measure how much your baby is sucking from your breast, but other signs will indicate how the two of you are doing:

- When the room is quiet, you will hear your baby swallowing.

- Once your milk has arrived, you may notice that your breasts soften during a feeding as they are emptied of milk.

- After the first four or five days, you should be changing six to eight wet diapers each day. In addition, you will notice one or several small, dark-green stools—sometimes one after every feeding—that become lighter after the first (meconium) stools are passed. As your milk supply becomes well established, your baby's stools will take on a yellowish color and a soft or runny consistency. Later on, stools typically become less frequent.

- Tracking your baby's weight will give you specific and important information. *It is normal for a baby to drop nearly 10 percent of her birth weight—about eleven or twelve ounces, for example, for a seven-pound baby (0.31 to 0.34 kg for a baby weighing 3.2 kg)—during the first week.* Usually she will have returned to her birth weight by two weeks of age, and thereafter she should gain about two-thirds to one ounce (or about 20 to 30 grams) per day. Obviously, you can't track these small changes at home on the bathroom scale. Instead, it is common to have a checkup during the first week or two after birth, during which your baby will be weighed on a scale that can detect smaller changes. If there is any question about appropriate weight gain, your doctor will ask you to return every week (or more often, if needed) to follow her progress. Some physicians' offices allow mothers to bring in their newborns for a quick "weigh-in" without charging for the visit.

One of the most important—and hardest—things to remember if you are concerned about the adequacy of your nursing is to *relax*. If you approach every feeding with fear and trembling, you may have difficulty with your let-down reflex. Furthermore, newborns seem to have an uncanny sense of Mom's anxiety, and their jittery response may interfere with smooth latching on and sucking. Remember that for many women, breastfeeding requires time, effort, and learning. Even if your first few feedings seem awkward or your baby doesn't seem to be getting the hang of it immediately, you should be able to make this process work.

What do I do if my baby wants to nurse all the time?

All babies derive comfort and satisfaction from sucking, but some are true enthusiasts who would be more than happy to turn every nursing session into a ninety-minute marathon. You may be happy with this arrangement, but more likely it can lead to sore nipples and a gnawing concern that your entire existence has been reduced to being a mobile restaurant. Fortunately, you are not without options.

A healthy newborn, properly attached to the breast and sucking continuously, will empty about 90 percent of the milk available on each side within ten minutes. You can usually hear and feel the transition from intense sucking and swallowing to a more relaxed, pacifying sucking after five to ten minutes on each side, at which point you can decide how long you want to continue. If you're both feeling cozy and comfortable, relax and enjoy it. But if it's the middle of the night and you need sleep, or other children need your attention, or you're getting sore, you won't destroy your baby's personality by gently detaching her.

A problem can arise, however, if your baby sounds terribly unhappy and indignant when you decide enough's enough. How do you respond? The answer depends on how far along and how well established you are in your nursing relationship. In the earliest days when milk is just arriving or you're not sure whether she is truly swallowing an adequate volume, it is probably better to give her the benefit of the doubt and continue for a while longer. This is especially true if you are blessed with a casual "gourmet" or "suck and snooze" baby who may not empty your breast very quickly.

But watch the indicators of your progress: good swallowing sounds, frequent wet diapers, weight gain, and softening of your breast after feeding. If you notice these and feel you have developed a smooth nursing routine after two or three weeks, you can consider other calming maneuvers, including the use of a pacifier. *If your soothing maneuvers aren't working, however, or your baby doesn't seem to be gaining weight, contact your baby's doctor for further evaluation and recommendations.*

Some mothers make the mistake of assuming that every sound from a baby should be answered with nursing, when something else (or nothing in particular) may be bothering her. If, for example, she just finished a good feeding thirty minutes ago and begins to fuss after being put down for a nap, it is reasonable to wait and listen for a while, since she may settle down on her own, rather than trying to nurse her again. As the days pass, you will become more discerning about the meaning of your baby's various crying messages.

A final note: If you are having a significant problem with breast-feeding, seek out a lactation consultant for a wealth of knowledge and practical suggestions.

What are the basics of formula feeding?

First things first: *For the first year, do not feed your baby cow's milk from the dairy section at the store.* Cow's milk that has not been specifically modified for use in infant formulas is not digested well by human infants; it contains significant loads of protein that your baby's kidneys will have difficulty processing, and it contains inadequate amounts of vitamin C, vitamin E, and iron. It also contains inadequate amounts of fat, which provides 50 percent of the calories in human milk and formula, and the fat that is present may be more difficult for the baby to digest and absorb. Furthermore, the new baby's intestine may be irritated by cow's milk, resulting in a gradual but potentially significant loss of red blood cells. This may lead to anemia, which in turn may be aggravated by an insufficient supply of iron. Finally, some of the protein in cow's milk may be absorbed through the baby's intestine in a way that can lead to allergy problems later in life.

The vast majority of bottle-fed infants are given iron-fortified commercial formulas, whose manufacturers have gone to great lengths to match mother's milk as closely as possible. The most commonly used formulas are based on cow's milk that has been *significantly* altered for human consumption. Among other things, the protein is made more digestible and less allergenic, lactose is added to match that of human milk, and butterfat is removed and replaced with a combination of other fats more readily absorbed by infants.

Soy formulas are based on soy protein and do not contain lactose, which is the main carbohydrate in cow's milk. These are used for the small percentage of infants who are allergic to the protein in cow's milk or (much less commonly) cannot digest lactose and thus develop excessive gas, cramps, and diarrhea when they consume regular formula.

In addition, bottle-fed infants who have diarrhea resulting from a viral or bacterial infection may develop a temporary difficulty processing lactose. During their recovery, these babies may tolerate soy formulas better than cow's milk formulas. Infants from families with a strong history of cow's milk allergy have traditionally been started on soy formulas as a precautionary measure. However, this has not been shown to prevent the development of cow's milk allergy, and up to 50 percent of infants who are allergic to cow's milk will prove to be allergic to soy formula as well. Furthermore, because of some subtle differences between the protein in soy and cow's milk, as well as a tendency for calcium and certain other minerals to be absorbed less efficiently from soy milk, soy-based formulas should be reserved for full-term infants who are clearly intolerant of cow's milk. Soy formulas should *not* be fed to premature infants.

There are a variety of formulas that have been designed for special needs. Infants who are allergic to both cow's milk and soy formulas may use what are called protein hydrolysate formulas, in which the proteins are essentially predigested. Special formulas are also available for babies with phenylketonuria (PKU) and for premature infants.

Check with your baby's physician regarding the type(s) of formula he or she recommends. Once you have made your choice, you can stock up with one or more of the three forms in which they are normally sold:

- **Ready-to-feed** is just that. Put it into a bottle if it isn't already packaged in one, make sure the temperature is right, and you're all set. While extremely convenient, this format is also the most expensive.

- **Concentrate** must be mixed with water in the exact amount recommended by the manufacturer. If it is too diluted (mixed with too much water), your baby will be shortchanged on nutrients. But if it is too concentrated (mixed with too little water), diarrhea and dehydration may result. The unused portion of an opened can of concentrate may be sealed and stored in the refrigerator for twenty-four hours, after which it should be discarded.

- **Powdered formula** is the least expensive form and must be mixed exactly as recommended, using the measuring scoop provided. A bottle of formula prepared from powder can be kept in the refrigerator for up to twenty-four hours and then should be discarded.

Whatever type of formula you use, be sure to check the expiration date on the bottle or can before feeding it to your baby.

In order to prevent your baby's formula from being contaminated by potentially harmful bacteria, it's important to take some basic precautions during preparation:

- Wash your hands before you begin handling formula, water, bottles, and nipples.

- If the formula you are using comes from a can, wipe the top before you open it. Use a separate can opener specifically designated for this purpose, and clean it on a regular basis.

- What about sterilizing bottles and nipples, and boiling water to be used in mixing formula? Over the past few decades the health-advisory pendulum has swung from boiling everything that might come near the baby's mouth to a more relaxed approach—using tap water for formula and hot soapy water or the dishwasher for bottles and nipples—and now more recently back again to more rigorous measures. While the vast majority of public water supplies in the United States are safe, an infant—especially during his first few weeks—is more vulnerable to infectious organisms, and protecting him is worth a little extra effort to boil the water you plan to mix with concentrated or powdered formula. A couple of minutes should be adequate; then let it cool. Bottled water should also be boiled unless it is specifically labeled as sterile.

- Well water should be checked for bacterial contamination and should always be boiled before you use it. In addition, well water may contain nitrates, components of plants, and fertilizers that can be toxic to infants, especially those younger than three months of age. If a well is your water source, have it tested on a regular basis for nitrate content before using it to mix formula for your baby. When in doubt, it would be best to use ready-to-feed formula or to mix bottled water with concentrated or powdered formula.

• Similarly, bottles, nipples, and utensils should be boiled for ten minutes before formula is prepared, although automatic dishwashers in which the water temperature reaches at least 180°F (82°C) appear to do an adequate job of sterilizing.[4] (Check your dishwasher's manual to confirm that your machine heats the water sufficiently to sterilize baby items.) After each use, bottles and nipple assemblies should be washed with hot, soapy water, using a bottle brush to clean the inside thoroughly, and then rinsed out. They can then be boiled or run through the dishwasher prior to the next time they are used for a feeding.

You can prepare a day's worth of bottles at one time, storing the ones you don't immediately need in the refrigerator for up to twenty-four hours. It's not necessary to warm a bottle, although younger babies prefer tepid or room-temperature formula. To warm a bottle you've stored in the refrigerator, let it sit for a few minutes in hot water. Warming the bottle in a microwave is *not* recommended because uneven heating may cause pockets of milk hot enough to scald a baby's mouth. Before feeding, shake the bottle well and let a drop or two fall on your hand. It should be barely warm and definitely not hot. Also check the flow rate from the nipple. An ideal flow is about one drop per second when the bottle is held upside down. If the nipple allows milk to flow too quickly, your baby may choke on it. If it flows too slowly, he may swallow air while he tries to suck out his meal.

You can use four- or eight-ounce (120 or 240 ml) bottles made from BPA-free plastic or glass. (Later on, however, when he can hold his own bottle, glass bottles should be replaced with plastic.) Many parents prefer the nurser style in which formula is poured into a plastic bag that attaches to a plastic shell and nipple assembly. Babies tend to swallow less air from the bags, but they cost more in the long run. It is important not to use the bags to mix concentrate or powder formula because you cannot measure accurately with them.

As with breastfeeding, bottle-feeding should be relaxed and unhurried, preferably in a comfortable and quiet area of your home. Hold your baby across your lap with his upper body slightly raised and his head supported. A flat position during feedings not only increases the risk of choking but also allows milk to flow into the passageways, called eustachian tubes, that lead into the middle ears. Frequent ear infections may result. Stroke the nipple across his cheek or lower lip to start the rooting reflex, and be sure to keep the bottle elevated enough so the milk completely covers the inside of the nipple. Otherwise he may start sucking air.

The fact that milk is flowing from a bottle does not mean that the feeding should switch to autopilot. Take time to lock eyes with your infant, talk or sing softly to him, gently caress him, and pray about this new life with which you've been entrusted. Your baby should not be left unattended with a bottle propped in his mouth. This practice puts your baby at an unnecessary risk for ear infections or choking.

Formula-fed newborns typically will consume two or three ounces (60 to 90 ml) every two to four hours, gradually increasing to a routine of taking about three to four ounces (90 to 120 ml) every four hours by the end of the first month. The amount per feeding will then increase by about an ounce every month, up to a maximum of eight ounces (240 ml) at a time. A general rule of thumb is that a normal baby will need between two and two and one-half ounces of formula per pound of body weight each day (up to fifteen pounds), with a maximum of thirty-two ounces of formula per day. (In metric equivalents, that would be about 130 to 165 ml of formula per kilogram, up to 6.8 kg, with a maximum of 960 ml of formula per day.) As we noted earlier, normally he will give a number of cues (such as looking more alert, fidgeting, or sucking on his hand) when he is hungry—remember that crying is a *late* sign of hunger—and will turn his head away or push the nipple out of his mouth with his tongue when he is full. If the bottle isn't empty, don't force the issue. However, during the first few weeks, it is wise to awaken him to feed if he is sleeping for stretches of more than four or five hours during the day.

As with breastfeeding, every baby's pattern of bottle-feeding (both in timing and amounts of formula taken) will be a little different. It's more important to become familiar with your own baby's cues for being hungry or full rather than trying to follow a particular formula (no pun intended) to the letter. If you're wondering whether he is getting enough, or if you're concerned that he seems to want too much, by all means have him checked by your physician. It will help if you keep a simple log—how much formula he is taking and when, and how many wet diapers you are changing every day—for a couple of days before the visit.

I thought newborns spent most of their time sleeping. Why does mine wake so frequently?

During the first three months, a baby's sleeping patterns are quite different from those she will experience the rest of her life. A newborn sleeps anywhere from twelve to eighteen hours every day, but this is not unbroken slumber. Her small stomach capacity and her round-the-clock need for nutrients to fuel her rapid growth essentially guarantee that her life will consist of ongoing three- or four-hour cycles of feeding, wakefulness, and sleep. Like it or not, two or three feedings will be on the nighttime agenda for the first several weeks.

Furthermore, the patterns of brain activity during sleep are unique in a newborn, such that a new baby who has just fallen asleep may be easily awakened for twenty minutes or more, until she moves into her phases of deeper sleep. This accounts for those character-building situations for some parents in which they feel they are dealing with a little time bomb with a short fuse. A fed, dry, and apparently tired baby fusses and resists but finally succumbs to sleep after prolonged cuddling and rocking. But when placed ever so gently into the cradle or crib, she suddenly startles and sounds off like a fire alarm. The cycle repeats over and over until everyone, baby included, is thoroughly exhausted and frustrated. The problem is that this baby isn't getting past her initial sleep phase and happens to be one who is easily aroused out of it. If all else fails, the problem usually will resolve itself by the age of three months.

How do I help my baby enter the "slumber zone"?

Given the unique characteristics of a newborn's sleep, two basic but quite different approaches to helping newborns fall asleep have developed. Each approach has advocates who tend to view their ideas as vital to a happy, stable life for both parent and child, while seeing the other as producing troubled, insecure babies. In reality, both have something to offer, and neither will work for every baby-parent combination.

One method calls for parents to be intimately and directly involved in all phases of their baby's sleep. Proponents of this approach recommend that she be nursed, cuddled, rocked, and held continuously until she has been asleep for at least twenty minutes. She can then be put down in her customary sleeping place, which may be Mom and Dad's bed. The primary advantage of this approach is that it can help a baby navigate through drowsiness and active sleep in the comfort and security of closeness to one or both parents. Those who favor this approach claim that a baby does best when she has more or less continuous contact with a warm body, having just exited from inside of one. Those who challenge this approach argue that she may become so accustomed to being "manipulated" into sleep that she will not be able to fall asleep on her own for months or even years.

The other approach suggests that a baby can and should learn to "self-calm" and fall asleep on her own. Rather than nursing her to sleep, she can be fed thirty to sixty minutes before nap or bedtime and then put down before she is asleep. She may seem restless for fifteen or twenty minutes or even begin crying but will likely settle and fall asleep if left alone. Proponents of self-calming feel this approach frees Mom and Dad from hours of effort to settle their baby and allows the baby to become more flexible and independent without her security being dependent on their immediate presence at all times. Critics argue that leaving her alone in a bassinet or crib represents cruel and unusual treatment at such a young age. Some even suggest that this repeated separation from parental closeness leads to sleep disorders (or worse) later in life.

You may be relieved to know that neither of these methods was carved in stone on Mount Sinai along with the Ten Commandments. You should tailor your approach to your baby's unique temperament and style and to your (and your family's) needs.

Most babies give clues when they are ready to sleep—yawning, droopy eyelids, fussiness—and you will want to become familiar with your child's particular signals. If she is giving you these cues, lay her down in a quiet, dimly lit setting and see if she will fall asleep. If she is clearly unhappy after fifteen or twenty minutes, check on her. Assuming that she is fed and dry, comfort her for a while and try again. If your baby is having problems settling herself, especially during the first few weeks, do not attempt to "train" her to do so by letting her cry for long periods of time. *During the first few months, it is unwise, for many reasons, to let a baby cry indefinitely without tending to her. Babies at this stage of life are not capable of being manipulative and cannot be "spoiled" by adults who are very attentive to their needs.*

If you need to help your new baby transition into quiet sleep, any of these time-honored methods may help:

- Nursing (or a bottle, if using formula) may help induce sleep, especially at the end of the day. However,

    (a) Don't overfeed with formula or, worse, introduce solids such as cereal at this age in hopes of inducing a long snooze. A stomach that is too full will interfere with sleep as much as an empty one. Solids are inappropriate at this age and will not lengthen sleep.

    (b) Never put a baby to bed with a bottle propped in her mouth. Not only can this lead to a choking accident, but it also allows milk to flow into her eustachian tubes (which lead into the middle ears), increasing her risk of ear infections. (Also, an older baby who has become accustomed to going to bed with a bottle of milk or juice will be at risk for developing tooth decay.)

- Rocking gently while you cuddle your baby can calm both of you. If this works for your baby, relax and enjoy it. A comfortable rocking chair is a good investment, by the way, if one hasn't been handed down from earlier generations of your family.

- One alternative to the rocking chair is a cradle—again, rocked smoothly and gently. Another alternative is a baby swing, but it must be one that is appropriately designed for this age-group.

- Many new babies settle more easily if they are swaddled—wrapped snugly in a light blanket.

- Quiet sounds such as the whirring of a small fan (not aimed toward the baby), a CD recording of the ocean or soft lullabies, or even small devices that generate monotonous "white noise" may help settle your baby and screen out other sounds in the home.

- A gentle touch, pat, or massage may help settle a baby who is drowsy in your arms but squirmy in her bed.

- The gentle vibrations of a car ride are often effective at inducing a baby to fall asleep—though this should be considered only as a last-resort maneuver for a very difficult sleeper.

In some situations, prolonged rocking, jostling, patting, and singing may be counterproductive, keeping a baby awake when she needs *less* stimulation in order to settle down. If a few weeks of heroic efforts to induce sleep don't seem to be working, it may be time to take another look at self-calming. Steps that may help the self-calming process when a baby has been put down but is not yet asleep include the following:

- Guide a baby's flailing hand toward her mouth. Many infants settle effectively by sucking on their hand or fingers.

- Identify a simple visual target for the baby's gaze, such as a single-colored surface; a small, nonbreakable mirror in her crib; or a nearby window or night-light, and place her in a position where she can see it. (Complex visual targets such as moving mobiles or busy patterns may not be as useful for settling during the earliest weeks, especially when a baby is very tired.)

- Make sure she is on her back before falling asleep. This is an important measure to help prevent the tragedy of sudden infant death syndrome (SIDS).

What about sleeping through the night?

Newborns do not typically sleep in long stretches during the first several weeks, nor do they know the difference between day and night. By two months, however, they are capable of lasting for longer periods without a feeding. Most parents will go through the pulse-quickening experience of awakening at dawn and realizing that the baby didn't sound off in the middle of the night. "Is he okay?" is the first breathless concern, followed by both relief and quiet exultation: "He slept through the night!"

By three months of age, much to their parents' relief, a majority of babies have established a regular pattern of uninterrupted sleep for seven or eight hours each night. However, some will take longer to reach this milestone. A few actually drift in the wrong direction, sleeping peacefully through most of the day and then snapping wide-awake—often fidgeting and fussing—just when bleary-eyed parents are longing for some rest. If you have a baby who favors the wee hours, you will want to give him some gentle but definite nudges to use the night for sleeping:

- Make a specific effort to increase his awake time during the day. Don't let him fall asleep during or right after eating, but instead provide some gentle stimulation. Talk or sing to him, lock eyes, change his clothes, play with his hands and feet, rub his back, or let Grandma coo over him. Don't make loud noises to startle him, and do not under any circumstances shake him. (Sudden movements of a baby's head can cause physical damage to the brain.) Let him nap only after he has been awake for a while after nursing. This can also help prevent a baby from becoming dependent on a feeding to fall asleep.

• If your baby is sleeping for long periods during the day and fitfully at night, consider gently awakening him while he is in one of his active sleep phases when a nap has lasted more than three or four hours.

• By contrast, make nighttime interactions—especially those middle-of-the-night feedings—incredibly boring. Keep the lights low, the conversation minimal, and the diaper change (if needed) businesslike. This is not the time to party.

• Remember that babies frequently squirm, grunt, and even seem to awaken briefly during their active sleep phases. Try to avoid intervening and interacting with him during these times because you may unknowingly awaken your baby when he was just shifting gears into the next phase of sleep. This may require some adjusting of your sleeping arrangements.

• If your baby tends to awaken by the dawn's early light and you don't care to do likewise, try installing shades or blinds to block out the first rays of sunlight. Don't assume that his rustling around in bed necessarily means he is waking up for good. Wait for a while before tending to him because he may go back to sleep.

• During these early weeks of nighttime feedings and day-time naps, it may be necessary to "sleep when the baby sleeps" in order to get an adequate amount of rest. This may be challenging when there are other tasks that need to be done. But if you're exhausted, your baby's daytime naps may be a much-needed opportunity to recharge your own batteries. You may even try to synchronize your newborn's and older sibling's naptime(s). If you succeed, give yourself permission to turn off the phone and lie down.

What about sudden infant death syndrome (SIDS)?

Sudden infant death syndrome (SIDS), also called crib death, has been the subject of intense research for a number of years. SIDS remains the most common cause of death between the age of one and twelve months in the U.S., claiming more than two thousand very young lives every year. While the exact cause is uncertain, SIDS appears to represent a disturbance of breathing regulation during sleep.

SIDS occurs most often between the first and fourth months, with a peak incidence between the second and third months. Ninety percent of cases occur by the age of six months. It is more common in the fall and winter months, perhaps because (at least in some cases) parents overcompensate for cold weather by over-heating an infant's room and increasing the layers of clothing and blankets in his sleeping environment. Also, colds and flu, which occur prior to SIDS in a significant number of cases, are more common at this time of year.

SIDS is more common in males with low birth weight and in premature infants of both sexes. African American and Native American infants are two to three times more likely to die from SIDS than white infants. Breast-fed babies, on the other hand, may have a reduced risk. In addition, some potential contributing factors to SIDS can be minimized by taking a few basic preventive measures:

- *Stay completely away from cigarettes during pregnancy, and don't allow anyone to smoke in your home after your baby is born.*

- *Lay your baby down on his back.* For decades, child-care guidebooks recommended that new babies sleep on their stomachs, based on the assumption that this would prevent them from choking on any material they might unexpectedly spit up. However, recent evidence suggests that this position might be a risk factor for SIDS. Therefore, it is now recommended that *a newborn be positioned on his back to sleep.* Since the 1994 initiation of the Back to Sleep campaign—a program designed to spread the word to professionals and parents alike that young infants should sleep on their backs—the number of SIDS deaths in the United States has dropped by 40 percent. Similar results have been observed in other countries. Exceptions to this guideline are made for premature infants, as well as for some infants with deformities of the face that might cause difficulty breathing when lying face up. In addition, your doctor may advise against the face-up position if your baby spits up excessively. If you have any question about sleeping position, check with your baby's doctor. Sometime after four months of age, your baby will begin rolling over on his own, at which point he will determine his own sleeping positions. By this age, fortunately, SIDS is extremely rare.

- *Put your baby to sleep on a safe surface.* Don't place pillows or any soft bedding material other than a fitted sheet under the baby. His head or face might become accidentally buried in the soft folds (especially if he happens to be face-down), which could lead to suffocation. Sheepskin, down mattresses, and feather beds pose a similar risk. For similar reasons don't put your baby to sleep on a wavy waterbed or beanbag chair. Even on one of these plastic surfaces, a baby whose face shifts to the wrong position could suffocate.

- *Don't overbundle your baby.* Overcompensating for the cold of winter by turning up the thermostat and wrapping a baby in several layers of clothing should be avoided. If he looks or feels hot and sweaty, start peeling off layers until he appears more comfortable.

- *Offer your baby a clean, dry pacifier when she is going to sleep.* A convincing body of recent research has associated pacifier use with a dramatic reduction in the risk of SIDS.

Where should my baby sleep?

By the time your baby arrives home for the first night, you will have had to address a basic question: Will she sleep in her own room, in a cradle or bassinet next to your bed, or in your bed right next to you? There are advocates for each of these arrangements.

Those who espouse sleeping with your baby (often called co-sleeping or shared sleep) point out that this is widely practiced throughout the world and claim that it enhances parent-infant bonding, facilitates breastfeeding, and gives the newborn a sense of security and comfort she won't feel in a crib. Shared-sleep advocates also argue that this practice reduces the risk of sudden infant death syndrome (SIDS), although the National Institute of Child Health and Human Development states that there is no scientific proof to support this claim.[5]

Furthermore, in 2002, the US Consumer Product Safety Commission (CPSC) issued a warning about the potential hazards of infants sleeping in adult beds, citing reports of more than one hundred deaths of children under the age of two during a three-year period.[6] Proponents of shared sleep contended that the CPSC's information was misleading and that this arrangement is safe if certain safety guidelines are followed. In any event, it is critical that parents who desire to share their bed with an infant take careful note of the following precautions:

- Use a wide bed with a firm mattress. Do not sleep with your baby on a water bed, sofa, or beanbag chair.

- Do not use fluffy bedding or cover your baby with your comforter.

- Your baby must sleep on her back (see page 42).

- Be sure there are no gaps between the mattress and a wall or bed frame in which your baby may be trapped.

- Your baby should sleep next to her mother but not between mother and father.

- If your baby will be positioned on the side of the mattress, use a mesh guardrail that fits flush against the mattress to prevent her from falling out of bed.

- Never sleep with your baby if you are using alcohol, sedatives, sleeping pills, or any medication that might affect your ability to awaken.

- Don't sleep with your baby if you're a smoker. The risk of sudden infant death syndrome associated with shared sleep is significantly higher among smokers.

- Older siblings or babysitters should not sleep with your baby.

- Don't leave a baby unattended in an adult bed.

Critics of shared sleep have also raised other concerns about the potential disruption of parental sleep, intimacy, and privacy. New babies don't quietly nod off to sleep at 10 p.m. and wake up calmly eight hours later. They also don't typically sleep silently during the few hours between feedings. As they pass through their active sleep phases, they tend to move around and make all sorts of noises, often sounding as if they're waking up. All of this activity isn't easy to ignore, especially for new parents who tend to be tuned in and concerned, if not downright worried, about how their new arrival is doing. Unless you learn to screen out these distractions and respond to your infant only when she is truly awake and in need of your attention, you may find yourself woefully short on sleep and patience within a few days.

The other issue to consider is the effect on the mother and father's relationship. If Mom and Dad are equally enthused about having a new bedmate, great. But many young couples aren't prepared for the demands a new baby may place on them and especially on a mother who may have little energy left at the end of the day for maintaining her relationship with her husband. A father who feels that his wife's attention is already consumed by the baby's needs may begin to feel completely displaced if the baby is in their bed too.

Many parents prefer to place their newborn in a cradle next to their bed. This arrangement allows for both a safe sleep environment and a close proximity to Mom that facilitates breastfeeding. The baby can be fed when she first becomes aroused by hunger, though parents may find themselves awakened repeatedly through the night by their baby's assorted movements and noises during sleep. They will also have to fine-tune their responses in order to avoid intervening too quickly during a restless period, which can accidentally interrupt a baby's transition from active to quiet sleep.

Parents who are contemplating having their baby sleep in another room (whether during the newborn period or after the first few months) may wonder whether they will hear her if she needs them. They can be assured that an infant who is truly awake, hungry, and crying during the night is difficult to ignore. And new parents, especially moms, are uniquely tuned in to their baby's nighttime vocalizing: They will normally awaken at the first sounds of crying, even after sleeping through louder sounds such as the rumble of a passing truck. On the other hand, crying is a late sign of hunger in the newborn, and it is often easier (for all concerned) if you nurse or feed an infant before she reaches a point of frantic crying.

You will need to determine which sleeping arrangements work best for your family and be flexible about the various possibilities. Moreover, it is important that parents continue to communicate openly with one another about this subject.

What if my baby won't stop crying?

One of the greatest mental and emotional adjustments new parents must make is sorting out the meanings of, and their responses to, the new baby's crying. In most cases, crying is a clear signal that a stomach is empty or a diaper full, and the appropriate response will quiet it. Even in these routine circumstances, however, the newborn cry has distinct qualities—insistent, edgy, and downright irritating. Indeed, it can sound almost like an accusation—"I don't like the care you're giving me!"

If your new baby's cry gives you a twinge of discomfort or even annoyance, don't panic; your response is quite normal. If you're a mother acutely short on sleep and sore in body (especially if you've had a cesarean delivery), with hormones shifting in all directions, you may find yourself harboring some troubling thoughts about your crying newborn. These feelings can enter the minds of even the most dedicated parents.

How should you feel about and deal with your baby's crying? First of all, it's important to understand the function of crying. Remember that a newborn baby is totally helpless and cannot do *anything* for himself other than suck on a breast or bottle given to him (or one or two of his own fingers that have accidentally found their way into his mouth). Unless someone meets his most basic needs on an ongoing basis, he will not survive. Crying is his only means—but a most effective one—of provoking a parent into action. It's *designed* to be annoying and irritating, to create all sorts of unpleasant feelings, especially among those closest to him. The responses that usually stop the crying—food, clean diapers and clothing, cuddling and cooing—are what keep him alive.

What does my baby's crying mean?

During these first three months, assume that when he cries, it's for a good reason. His crying is definitely not a deliberate effort to irritate you, manipulate you, or test parental limits. Therefore, it is appropriate to take action in response to your baby's crying, as opposed to ignoring it and hoping it will go away. *You cannot spoil a baby at this young age*, and for now it is far better to err on the side of giving too much attention than too little. He needs comfort, open arms, and ongoing love from those around him, even though he cannot express any signs of gratitude or even pleasure in response to all you give him. This is not the time for any misguided attempts to "train, mold, and discipline" your child. (In several months you will begin to have plenty of opportunities to carry out that important assignment.)

What is your baby trying to tell you when he cries? Most likely, one of these things:

- He's hungry and wants to be fed.

- He has a wet or dirty diaper.

- He's wet, hot, cold, or uncomfortable in some other way.

- He wants to be held.

- He's ready to go to sleep.

- He's had too much stimulation and needs a quieter environment for a while.

At some point, usually between two weeks and three months, there will be at least one occasion when you suspect that something has gone terribly wrong. Just a day or so ago you could comfort your baby regularly and predictably. A feeding every few hours, dry diapers, and a little rocking and cooing would end crying fairly quickly. Now, however, he starts fussing late in the afternoon or early in the evening, and nothing works for an hour . . . or two . . . or three. Or he suddenly lets out an ear-piercing wail or screams for no apparent reason in the middle of the night. What's going on? You may never know for sure. But it may help if you understand that many babies cry like this now and then, some do it every day, and a few seem determined to set a world's record for the longest crying episode in history.

What is colic?

According to a long-standing definition, if your baby cries three hours a day three days a week for three weeks, and he's between two weeks and three months of age, he has colic. True colicky episodes tend to occur around the same time each day, usually in the late afternoon or evening, and are marked by intense activity on the baby's part, such as flailing about or pulling his knees to his chest. From all appearances, he acts like he's feeling a lot of discomfort—and undoubtedly he is.

The classic theories about the cause of colic have assumed that the baby's intestinal tract is at fault—that it goes into uncontrollable spasms, perhaps because of immaturity or a reaction to something in Mom's milk or the current formula. Other proposed explanations include a problem interacting with parents, often assuming that Mother is tense or high-strung, and as a result the baby is also. But changing feeding patterns or formulas may or may not help, and colicky babies may land in families that are intact or disjointed, relaxed or uptight. Basically, a universal cause for colic has yet to be determined.

If your baby begins having long stretches of crying, you will need to address two basic concerns:

- Does he have a medical problem?

- How is everyone—baby included—going to get through this?

The first question needs to be answered relatively quickly, because a medical illness can be a much more serious problem during the first three months than when the baby is older. Some indicators of a disturbance that might need a physician's care include:

- Any fever over 100.4°F taken with a rectal thermometer

- Poor sucking at the breast or bottle

- Change in color from normal pink to pale or bluish (called cyanosis) during feeding or crying

- Overt vomiting, as opposed to spitting up. (When a baby spits up, the partially digested food burps into his mouth and dribbles down his chin and clothes. When he vomits, this material becomes airborne.)

- A marked increase in the amount and looseness of bowel movements

- Unusual jerking movements of the head, eyes, or other muscles that you don't recall seeing before

If any of these occur, you should contact your physician, and your baby should be checked—especially if he has a fever. If he is crying up a storm but seems okay otherwise, he should still have a medical evaluation, either as part of a routine checkup or at an appointment specifically for this purpose. The more specific information you can give the doctor, the better. When did the crying start? How long does it last? Does anything seem to set it off? Is it improved or worsened after a feeding? Are there any other symptoms?

Assuming your baby is doing well otherwise (gaining weight, arriving at his developmental milestones more or less on time, showing no apparent signs of medical illness), your primary tasks during his crying episodes are to *be there* for him and to make ongoing efforts to comfort him. *You are not a failure, and you should not give up if your measures do not succeed in stopping the crying.* Eventually each crying episode will end, and the crying season overall will come to a close, in nearly all cases by the third to fourth month of age.

What can I do for my colicky baby?

Assuming that he is fed, dry, and not sick, you can try any or all of the following, once or many times. If a particular measure helps one time but doesn't the next, don't panic. You may get impressive results today with something that failed miserably last week.

- **Soothing movements.** Gentle rocking or swaying in someone's arms is a time-honored baby comforter. Unfortunately, when a baby is wailing at full volume, you may unconsciously begin moving faster or more force-fully—but you should *avoid rapid, jerky movements*, which not only make the problem worse but may even injure the baby. Cradles and baby swings that support the body and head can also provide this type of movement.

- **Soothing sounds.** Provide humming, gentle singing, white noise, or pleasant recorded music.

- **Soothing positions.** Some colicky babies respond to being held tummy-down against your forearm like a football or across your thigh. Others seem to calm down while being carried close to Mom's or Dad's body in a baby sling. Swaddling in a light blanket and resting on one side or the other might help.

- **Soothing environments.** Spending time in a quiet, dimly lit room can help calm a baby who may be in sensory overload at the end of the day. Turn down the TV and unplug the phone if necessary.

- **Soothing trips.** A ride in the car or a stroller may provide the right mix of gentle movement and sound to soothe the crying.

- **Soothing touch.** Gentle touching or stroking of the back, stomach, or head may help.

- **Soothing sucking.** Nursing may seem to calm the crying, even if he just had a feeding. A pacifier may also work. If your baby doesn't seem satisfied by any of your feedings, you should check with his physician and possibly a lactation consultant as well. This is particularly important if he's not gaining adequate weight, because the problem may be that his hunger is never satisfied. If your colicky baby is formula-fed, you may at some point want to try a different brand or a different type of formula—for example, you might switch from cow's milk to soy-based formula. (Check with your baby's health-care provider on this.) Sometimes a change will bring about some noticeable improvement.

- **Self-soothing.** Sometimes all the rocking, singing, touching, and pacifying maneuvers unwittingly overload the baby's capacity to handle stimulation. The self-soothing measures mentioned in the previous section on sleep (pages 38–39) may work wonders when everything else has failed.

How can I handle the stress of trying to comfort a baby who always seems to be crying?

While all of this is going on:

- **Keep reminding yourself that "this too will surely pass."** You will deal with crying problems for only a short period of your child's life. Believe it or not, before you know it there will come a time when you'll wonder where all those baby years went.

- **If you find yourself reaching the end of your rope, don't take it out on the baby.** Mounting frustration and anger are indications that you need a brief time-out. If that time arrives, don't allow yourself to become a martyr or a child abuser. Sounding off verbally at the baby will accomplish nothing, and *you must not carry out any physical act of anger*—picking him up or putting him down roughly, shaking him, hitting him, or anything else that inflicts pain or injury—no matter how upset you may feel. Instead, put him in his cradle or crib and *walk away* for fifteen or twenty minutes until you have a chance to collect your thoughts and calm down. It won't hurt him to cry by himself for that period of time, and you can then try comforting him again. He may have expended enough energy to become more responsive to calming efforts at this point. If necessary, call a friend or relative and get your frustration off your chest, or let someone else come look after your baby for a while.

- **If at all possible, husband and wife should pass the baton during a prolonged crying episode.** Let Dad hold the baby while Mom takes a walk around the block and vice versa. Single moms—and for that matter, married ones—shouldn't be embarrassed to seek help from an experienced relative or friend. If Grandma wants to help you for a while during a rough evening, by all means let her do it. She may have a few tricks up her sleeve that aren't in any book.

- **Try to find some humor in all this to maintain your perspective.** Jot down some of your more humorous observations. If you have one or more books that have made you laugh out loud, by all means keep them close at hand.

- **Try to maintain "self-preservation" activities as much as possible.** A quiet time for reflection and prayer may have to occur during a feeding, but it will provide important perspective and strength. Having a world-class wailer is a humbling experience, and it is during these rough times that special intimacy with God often develops. The question to ask Him isn't "Why did You give me such a fussy baby?!" but "What do You want me to learn about myself and life in general through this experience?" You may be surprised at the answer.

- **If you have "gone the distance," repeatedly trying every measure listed here (and perhaps a few others as well) without success, check back with your baby's doctor.** Be prepared to give specific information—for example, how many hours the baby has been crying, not just "He won't stop!" Depending upon your situation and the baby's crying pattern, another medical evaluation may be in order.

In the first three months, when should my baby be seen for checkups?
Your pediatrician or family physician will ask that you follow a

specific routine of well-baby visits; there is a definite purpose to this plan that involves monitoring the baby's progress and administering immunizations that are very important to her health. If you have been sent home from the hospital within twenty-four hours of your baby's birth, your baby should be checked within the next twenty-four to forty-eight hours. If all is going smoothly, you can expect to take your baby back for a checkup between two and four weeks of age and then again at two months.

During these visits, the baby will be weighed and measured and the results plotted on a standardized growth chart, which allows the health-care provider to track her progress over time. You will be asked how she is feeding, sleeping, and eliminating urine and stool. At the one- and two-month visits, specific behavioral milestones such as smiling and head control will probably be discussed. The baby will be examined from head to toe, so be sure to put her in an outfit that can be removed easily.

It is important that you bring up any problems or concerns you have, no matter how minor they seem. If you have a number of questions, write them down and present them at the beginning of the visit so the practitioner can see what's on your mind. Don't suddenly pull them out as a list of "by the way" items after everything else is done. If the examiner seems rushed and uneasy about taking time to deal with your concerns, find out how and when you can go over them. Some large practices have well-trained nurses or other health educators who can answer most of the questions you might have.

Your physician will recommend that your baby receive a number of routine immunizations during her first three months. These will be given to protect her against a number of dangerous diseases—whooping cough (pertussis), diphtheria, tetanus, polio, rotavirus infection, and hepatitis B—as well as against pneumococcus and *Haemophilus influenzae* type B, bacteria that can cause meningitis, pneumonia, and other serious infections.

Many parents are anxious about the prospect of their tiny infant receiving these vaccines, and some have read literature suggesting that they are dangerous or ineffective. But overwhelming evidence indicates that immunizations do in fact drastically reduce the risk of your baby becoming ill with a number of serious or even fatal infections. And the odds of having a problem from any of the vaccines are far less than the odds of contracting the disease if no vaccine is given.

What if my baby becomes ill?

Because newborns normally receive a healthy donation of Mom's antibodies through the umbilical cord blood supply prior to birth, they usually escape common illnesses such as colds and flu during the first several weeks, as long as they are well nourished and their environment is kept reasonably clean. Nursing infants have the added advantage of ingesting their mother's antibodies at every feeding.

This is indeed providential because an illness in a baby younger than three months of age is a completely different situation from one in an older baby. For one thing, your new baby has very few ways to notify you that something is wrong. You will not have the luxury of language and specific complaints ("My ear hurts" or "I have a headache") to guide you. You won't have months or years of experience with this particular child—or, if this is your first baby, perhaps with any child—to sense what is "normal" for her.

In addition, your baby's defense system is still under construction, and her ability to fight off microscopic invaders will not be fully operational for a number of months. As a result, a seemingly minor infection acquired during the first several weeks can turn into a major biological war.

Also—and this is the most unsettling reality of all—an illness can go sour much more rapidly in a newborn than in older children. If bacteria are on the move, they can spread like wildfire. If fluids are being lost through vomiting or diarrhea, dehydration can develop over several hours rather than days.

These warnings are not meant to generate undue anxiety but rather to encourage you to notify your baby's health-care provider if you think something is wrong, especially during the first three months. You can also reduce your newborn's risk of infection by keeping her out of crowded public places, preventing if possible direct contact with individuals who are ill with contagious infections, and minimizing group child-care situations, especially during the first few weeks after birth.

What are the signs that my baby might have a problem?

Some of the danger signals in infants are similar to those that will alert you to problems later in life. But in newborns, several of these signals are more critical and require a more immediate and detailed evaluation than in older babies and children. Here are some important newborn distress signals:

Fever. There will be many occasions in the coming months and years when your child will feel hot, and the thermometer will agree. In babies over three months of age, this may or may not be cause for alarm, depending on what else is going on. *In a baby under three months of age, however, a rectal temperature over 100.4°F (38°C) should be considered cause for an immediate call to the doctor's office.*

If your baby seems perfectly well, his temperature is slightly above 100.4°F, and there is a possibility that he was overdressed or in a hot environment, you can remove some clothing and try taking his temperature again in thirty to forty-five minutes. A temperature that is closer to normal will be reassuring—but you should run the story by your baby's physician anyway. Do not give the baby acetaminophen (Tylenol) or a tepid bath in this situation because you need to know whether the fever will come down on its own. Besides, the fever itself is not dangerous. It is the possible causes of the fever that you need to worry about.

If there is no doubt about the presence of fever, your baby needs to be evaluated right away, either by his own physician or at the emergency room. You may be surprised or even alarmed by the number of tests that may be requested after your baby is examined. The problem is that a newborn fever can indicate a serious bacterial infection that could involve the lungs, urinary tract, or the tissues that surround the brain and spinal cord (these tissues are called meninges). Bacteria could also be present in the bloodstream, in which case the baby is said to have sepsis.

Feeding poorly. Lack of interest in nursing, poor sucking, or failing to awaken for feeding well beyond the expected time could be an important indicator of a medical problem. If you contact a physician with a concern that your newborn is ill, the physician will want to know, among other things, how the baby appears to be feeding.

Vomiting. As we will discuss later in this chapter, you will need to distinguish between spitting up and vomiting, since the latter is much more significant in a newborn.

Decreased activity or alertness. A baby who is listless—with eyes open but little spontaneous movement, an indifferent response to stimulation, or very floppy muscle tone—may be quite sick. Believe it or not, a vigorous protest by a baby during an examination is a reassuring finding. At this age, remaining quiet and disinterested while being poked and prodded by the doctor is not a sign of being a "good" patient but rather an indication of probable illness.

Nonstop crying. Many babies enter a "crying season" between two weeks and three months of age, without any specific medical cause. But you can't assume that prolonged, inconsolable crying is normal until the baby has been evaluated by his physician.

Abnormal movements. Unusual jerking of arms, legs, or head, especially if sustained for several seconds, may represent a seizure or other significant problem affecting the nervous system. Contact your baby's doctor immediately for further advice if you observe this type of activity.

Unusual color. A pale or mottled color of the skin or bluish discoloration of the lips could indicate a change in normal circulation patterns.

What are some common medical problems during a baby's first three months?

Jaundice. This is a yellow-orange discoloration of skin caused by the buildup of a substance called bilirubin in the bloodstream. Bilirubin is a by-product of the breakdown of red blood cells, which normally circulate for about four months until they wear out. (New red cells are constantly produced within the bones in tissue called marrow.) Removing and recycling the contents of red cells require the liver to process bilirubin, which before birth is largely managed through the mother's circulation. After birth, the newborn's liver takes a few days to gear up for this job, and the level of bilirubin in the bloodstream will increase by a modest amount. If a significant backlog of bilirubin develops, the baby's skin will take on a yellow-orange hue, beginning with the head and gradually spreading toward the legs.

Whether or not jaundice is significant will depend upon several factors, including the level of bilirubin, how soon and how fast it has risen, the suspected cause, and whether the baby was full-term or premature. In some instances, extremely high bilirubin levels can damage the central nervous system, especially in the premature infant. *Therefore, if you notice that your new baby's skin color is changing to pumpkin orange, the white area of the eyes is turning yellow, and/or your baby is feeding poorly, see your doctor immediately.*

If there is any concern, the doctor will order blood tests to check the bilirubin level, and other studies may be done to look for underlying causes. Normally the jaundice will resolve on its own, although some healthy babies will carry a slight yellow-orange tint for weeks. Occasionally pediatricians will recommend some form of treatment to help address this problem.

Colds and other respiratory infections. These types of illness are relatively uncommon in this age-group. The breathing patterns in a newborn baby, however, may cause you some concern. He will at times move air in and out noisily, with snorting and sniffing sounds emanating from his small nasal passages, even when they are completely dry. Some sneezing now and then isn't uncommon, but watery or thick drainage from one or both nostrils is definitely abnormal. A call to the doctor's office and usually an exam are in order when this "goop" appears in a baby under three months.

If your newborn has picked up a cold, you can gently suction the excess nasal drainage with a rubber-bulb syringe, since a clogged nose will cause some difficulty breathing while he is feeding. *Do not give any decongestant or cold preparations to a baby this young unless given very specific directions—not only what kind, but exactly how much—from your baby's physician.* (In general, research has suggested that such medications are not terribly effective in babies and young children.)

Even when his nose is clear, your baby's breathing rate may be somewhat erratic, varying with his activity and excitement level. A typical rate is thirty to forty times per minute, often with brief pauses, sighs, and then a quick succession of breaths. If he is quiet and consistently breathing fifty or more times per minute, however, he may have an infection or another problem with his lungs or heart. Flaring of the nostrils, an inward sucking motion of the spaces between the ribs, and exaggerated movement of the abdomen with each breath suggest that he may be working harder than usual to breathe. An occasional cough probably doesn't signal a major problem, but frequent or prolonged bouts of coughing should be investigated, especially if there are any other signs of illness.

Infections of the middle ear. An ear infection (known as otitis media) may complicate a cold in any baby, including a newborn. There are, however, no specific signs of this important problem in a young baby. (At this age, movement of the hands around the side of the head are random, and your baby cannot deliberately point to or try to touch any area that is bothering him.) Furthermore, an ear infection can be much more serious in this age-group. If he is acting ill, irritable, running a fever, or all of these, he will need to have his ears checked by his doctor.

Overflowing tears. Some babies always seem to be overflowing with tears in one eye. This is caused by a narrowing of the tear duct near the inner corner of each eye, which acts like a drain for the tears that are produced constantly to keep the eye moist. Aside from causing a nonstop trail of tears down one side of the face, this narrowing can lead to a local infection manifested by goopy, discolored drainage, crusting, and if more widespread, a generalized redness of the eye known as conjunctivitis. The crusting and drainage will need to be removed gently using moist cotton balls, which should be promptly thrown away after being used since they may be contaminated with bacteria. In addition, the baby's health-care provider will probably prescribe antibiotic eye drops or ointment for a few days. He or she may also suggest that you gently massage the area between the inner corner of the eye and the nose to help displace and move any mucous plug that might have formed.

Usually the clogged tear duct will eventually open on its own, but if it continues to be a problem after six months, talk to your baby's doctor, who may refer you to an ophthalmologist.

Spitting up or vomiting. Spitting up breast milk or formula is not uncommon during the first weeks after birth, and some babies return a little of their feedings for months, especially if they are not promptly burped. As long as he is otherwise doing well—gaining weight and making developmental progress—this can be considered a temporary annoyance that will correct itself. However, if a baby in this age-group begins vomiting, with stomach contents returning more forcefully, some prompt medical attention is in order.

If there is also a marked increase in the amount of stool (usually indicating that an infection has developed in the intestinal tract), the baby will need careful observation for signs of dehydration. These signs include poor feeding, a decrease in urine output (manifested by fewer wet diapers), sunken eyes, decreased tears or saliva, persistent fussiness or listlessness, and cool or mottled skin. A baby under three months of age with any of these problems should be evaluated immediately.

Projectile vomiting is an alarming event in which the stomach's contents fly an impressive distance. A young baby with this problem should be checked promptly. In a few cases, forceful vomiting is caused by a thickening of muscle in the portion of small intestine known as the pylorus, just past the stomach, which can begin to cause trouble after the baby's second week. This condition, known as pyloric stenosis, has traditionally been considered a problem of firstborn males, but a baby of either gender or any birth-order position can be affected. In a young baby with forceful vomiting, a combination of an examination with an ultrasound or an X-ray study of the stomach will usually clarify the diagnosis. If pyloric stenosis is present, surgical correction is a must and should be carried out as soon as possible. The surgery is relatively simple, however, and is very well tolerated by the vast majority of infants.

CHAPTER 3

THREE TO SIX MONTHS

AS YOUR BABY grows and slowly graduates from the newborn stage, you will find yourself entering a phase of increased enjoyment and satisfaction in parenting. During these months, your baby will progress from being a pure "taker" of your love and energy to a "giver" as well, someone who can flash a smile and carry on irresistible interactions with nearly anyone who will give him the time of day. For a baby, these months are full of intense exploration. No longer restricted to crying as his only method of gaining attention, your baby is now finding all sorts of new ways to investigate and affect what goes on around him. While he isn't exactly capable of propelling himself out the front door while your back is turned, his wondrous new skills will create some safety challenges.

How is my baby going to develop physically during the next few months?

During his first three months, one of your baby's major accomplishments was simply learning to keep his head still enough to focus on an object or track a moving object with his eyes.

Body in motion. Now your infant is starting to use larger muscle groups that will eventually allow him to sit up on his own. This begins with more decisive head control, which you will notice when he is lying on his stomach while awake. He will make a more deliberate effort to keep his head elevated so he can see what's going on in front of him. You can encourage the exercise of these upper back and neck muscles by placing a small toy or brightly colored object—or your smiling face—in front of him while he is in this position.

He will then progress to lifting his entire upper chest, with or without help from his arms. When he combines this with vigorous kicking, you will see surprisingly active rocking, and by five or six months, the right combination of movements will send him rolling over front to back. Rolling back to front will not be far behind. (A few babies roll back to front first.) Invariably, he will accomplish this skill for the first time when you least expect it, so never leave him alone on any elevated surface, such as a bed or changing table, or he may add free-falling to his new movement experiences.

At this stage he will enjoy being propped on pillows in a sitting position, although he must be watched because he can easily topple forward. He will soon figure out how to sit in a hunched position with one or both hands on the floor, precariously maintaining his balance. He can still topple easily, so make sure his landing will be on a soft surface. At six months of age at the earliest, he will be able to maintain a sitting position without using his hands, although he is still a few months away from maneuvering himself into a sitting position.

Another adventure for him at this age is being held by the upper body and "standing" in someone's lap. Most babies love to flex their legs and bounce up and down, as if ready to bear their weight in a standing position. They are, of course, nowhere near achieving this milestone, and the playful bouncing won't bring it along any sooner. But it also won't cause any harm to growing muscles and bones. However, you should not suspend or lift a baby's full weight by holding his hands or arms.

Your baby's ability to use his hands will develop dramatically during these three months. As a newborn, he spent most of his time with his little fists clenched and could only respond with a tight reflex grip to objects placed in his hands. Now he will spend more time with open palms, and more important, he will begin to reach deliberately toward interesting things that catch his eye. He will grasp as if his hand were in a mitten, thumb against the other fingers, or rake an item into his hand. (Independent use of the fingers and the ability to pick up an object between the thumb and index finger will not develop until about nine months of age.) You will not be able to tell whether he is right- or left-handed at this point, since this characteristic is not clearly manifested until about the age of three years.

But even without fine-tuning, your baby will become a first-class grabber by the age of six months. Not only will he reach for toys in his immediate vicinity (or his own feet), but when someone holds him, he will expertly seize hair, earrings, glasses, or the pen in Dad's shirt pocket. Furthermore, all of these items will be inspected carefully and fearlessly, not only with eyes and fingers but invariably with his mouth. You will now need to enter a state of perpetual vigilance for small objects that you would rather not see entering his mouth, either because they are disgusting or because they might be accidentally swallowed and block his airway.

As his reaching and grasping skills become more developed, he will also discover the joy of letting go. During these three months, you will see him transfer an object from one hand to the other, which requires that one hand release what the other hand takes. At some point he will also discover gravity, as he begins to drop things and observe what happens as a result. All of this activity is exploratory and not a sign of a destructive streak or a future career in sports.

Vision and hearing. During these three months, your baby will continue to gain in the ability to see and hear what's going on around her. By six months she will be able to focus on people or objects several feet away and follow movement in all directions. She will show interest in more complex patterns and subtle shades of color, so this is a great time to hang a mobile over her crib. (Make sure that she can't reach it, however—if she grasps it and pulls it loose, a mobile could fall on her or she could become entangled in its strings.) She will also find stroller rides stimulating times to take in a passing parade of new colors and shapes.

She will become more skillful at localizing the source of sounds and turning her head in the direction of your voice or an interesting noise in her vicinity. In addition, you will begin hearing a wider range of sounds—babbles, belly laughs, bubbling noises, and even a screech or two for good measure. Sometimes she will even alter her "speech" patterns, raising and lowering her voice as if giving an oration in a language only she understands. Rather than parroting back her assorted sounds, which is often irresistible, you can begin to transform some of her favorite syllables into simple words such as *baby*, *doggie*, and *Mommy* and feed them back to her. By seven months of age, she should begin imitating sounds you make.

How is my baby's social development going to change during these months?

For many parents, this stage of a baby's life is one of the most pleasant they will experience, a time when a true personality emerges from the seemingly endless cycles of feeding, sleeping, and crying during the first three months. All of her new skills in movement, vision, hearing, and noisemaking seem to converge and complement each other as she shows off for family, friends, and complete strangers.

In all of these encounters, your baby is finding out what kind of world she lives in. What sights and sounds envelop her, and what happens when she tries to make an impact, in her own way, on her surroundings? Does she see smiles and bright colors, hear laughter and pleasant voices, and feel hugs, kisses, and cuddling? Is she in a place that is safe physically and emotionally? Even during her first stirrings of independence, she is still completely helpless, depending on the adults around her for her physical needs and her most basic sense of security. She may not be able to understand your words, but she'll get a strong message about her importance to you and your family.

What should my baby be eating?

If your baby is nursing, he will typically need to fill his tank about five times a day and soon should be skipping the late-night feeding(s) if he isn't already. By six months, if he is waking up two or three times during the night, it is far more likely to be for reasons other than hunger.

Some mothers who are breastfeeding quite successfully will, for a variety of reasons, begin to think about shifting from breast to bottle before their baby reaches six months of age. If at all possible, however, continue nursing during these months. If you need to start or resume employment outside the home and cannot nurse your baby during work hours, you do not necessarily need to switch your baby entirely to formula. Depending upon your schedule and your baby's feeding patterns, you may be able to nurse before and after work and even express milk (which can be used at a later feeding) during the time you are away from home.

A formula-fed baby will similarly be consuming five bottles every day, each containing five to eight ounces (about 150 to 240 ml) of formula, depending on his weight. You can discuss the amount with your physician at the four- and six-month checkups, but a ballpark amount for a given feeding is an ounce of formula for every two pounds of weight (30 ml for every 900 g). By the way, it's too early to begin drinking from a cup at this age. That adventure can begin after your baby reaches the six-month mark.

Parents of babies in this age-group often wonder if this is a good time to introduce solid foods. Thirty years ago, physicians routinely advised parents to begin feeding their babies rice cereal at two months and then speedily progress to other types of foods. Your baby's grandmother may have started you on cereal practically from day one, and perhaps one of your friends has announced with some satisfaction that her baby is already taking all sorts of fruits and vegetables at two months of age. But consuming solids is not a sign of advanced intelligence or motor skills. In fact, there are reasons you don't need to be in any hurry to introduce solids before your baby is six months old:

- Breast milk or formula can supply all of the fluid, calories, and nutrients your baby needs for his first six months, and it is more easily digested than other foods.

- Babies who are fed solids early may develop food allergies.

- Solid foods are best managed by a baby who has some basic developmental skills in place.

What can I expect with my baby's first experience with solid foods?

While you don't need to be in a rush to start solids, most babies are given their first taste of foods other than breast milk or formula between four and six months of age. Like many other everyday concerns in child rearing, directions for introducing solids to babies were not included in the Ten Commandments. Even the American Academy of Pediatrics (AAP) acknowledges a difference of opinion among its own experts on this topic. The AAP's Section on Breastfeeding (a subcommittee that makes policy recommendations on this subject) recommends breastfeeding exclusively for the first six months, while its Committee on Nutrition proposes that other foods (if safe, nutritious, and age appropriate) can be introduced between four and six months of age. Needless to say, families have made this transition for thousands of years in thousands of ways, with or without the input and approval of panels of experts. What follows are basic guidelines to help you navigate this passage smoothly, along with a few cautions about certain foods and feeding practices that would best be avoided.

Before you decide to let your baby try something other than breast milk or formula, consider your timing. First, she should be ready developmentally.

- While sucking at the breast or bottle, a newborn first protrudes her tongue, pushing it against the nipple as she sucks and swallows. This tongue-thrusting reflex, which gradually subsides over the first six months, interferes with the process of taking food from a spoon and moving it to the throat, where it can be swallowed. A baby who repeatedly pushes her tongue against the spoon probably isn't ready for solids.

- Accepting food from a spoon is much easier for a baby who can control her head position, a skill that will be far better developed after six months than at three or four. A young baby whose head flops everywhere if not supported should be given more time with just breast or bottle.

- By six months of age, your baby will be happily grabbing everything in sight and putting whatever she finds into her mouth, an indication that she will find a spoon worth exploring as well.

- If a couple of teeth erupt before six months of age (the usual time of the first appearance of teeth), this in itself is not a sign that your baby is ready for pizza. Your baby won't use her teeth to chew food yet for some months. In fact, even if she doesn't have teeth at the six-month mark, she will be quite able to swallow the mushy solids you'll be feeding her.

The other timing question to consider is the specific setting of your baby's first experience with solids. Pick a time when you aren't going to be rushed or hassled, and silence the phone for good measure. Your baby shouldn't be tired, cranky, ravenously hungry, or completely full. Give her part of a feeding of breast milk or formula before you try the new stuff. *Remember that when you begin solids, they will only supplement milk feedings, not substitute for them*, so the normal feeding should be finished after whatever solid food she has eaten.

What should you start with? The general consensus is that rice cereal specifically formulated for babies is best. It is well absorbed, contains iron, and rarely causes allergic reactions. Whether pre-mixed in a jar or prepared by you with water or formula, it can be adjusted to whatever thickness your baby prefers. You should feed her from a small spoon and not a bottle with an enlarged hole in the nipple. If she sucks solids out of a bottle, she may get too much volume and become obese if this is done repeatedly. And she will delay learning how to swallow solids without sucking.

Offer her about half of a small baby spoonful (or use a small coffee spoon if you wish), which should total about a quarter teaspoon (one ml). She may not know what to do with your offering and may even appear to reject it with a grimace. Talk to her in soothing tones through the entire process. When she gets the hang of swallowing this amount, she will begin opening her mouth in anticipation of more. Aim for a total of about one tablespoon (15 ml) once a day, gradually increasing to two or three tablespoons (30 to 45 ml) per feeding once or twice per day. If she simply refuses or repeatedly thrusts her tongue, don't force her. This is not a moral issue or a contest of wills. Simply wait and try again in another week or two.

When two or three tablespoons of rice cereal are going down smoothly at one feeding, you can try other cereals. Oats and barley are good for the next round, but check with your baby's doctor before trying corn or wheat cereals, which may provoke digestive problems in some infants. After cereals have been successfully consumed for a few weeks, you can think about adding other foods to the mix. Either vegetables or fruits may be the next category you try, but vegetables may hold an advantage because they will not condition your baby to sweet tastes. Fruits can be added later, and meats should be introduced last. By the time your baby is eating from three or four food groups, she will probably be eating three times per day. You may choose to raise a vegetarian and not introduce meats to your baby at all, but if you do this, be sure that you are adequately informed so your baby won't be deprived of any necessary nutrients. Consult your pediatrician or a registered dietician for guidance in this area.

Let your baby try each new food (one to three tablespoons' worth or 15 to 45 ml) for a few days before introducing another. Observe her for any signs of a reaction: diarrhea, irritability, runny nose, coughing or wheezing, or a rash, especially around the face. If there is any possibility that a reaction has occurred, withdraw the food, wait for the problem to calm down, and try again. If you see the same response, put that food aside for several weeks and then run the story by your baby's doctor before serving it to her again. Of course, if any feeding is followed by a more severe reaction, such as an immediate rash or difficulty breathing, contact the doctor right away. Fortunately, sudden and intense reactions to foods are very uncommon at this age.

You can obtain many foods for your baby in prepackaged forms at the store, or you can prepare them yourself. Commercial baby foods have the advantage of convenience, especially if you are traveling or are short on time for food preparation. Unlike their predecessors of a few decades ago, most are free of sugar, salt, and artificial flavorings—they contain just the straight food in a mushy consistency, ready to feed. When opening a baby-food jar, make sure the safety button in the middle of the lid pops up. If it doesn't, return the jar or throw it away. No matter how the baby food is packaged, don't feed your baby directly out of the container because the enzymes and bacteria from her saliva may degrade or contaminate the food she doesn't finish. Instead, spoon a small amount onto a plate and refrigerate what remains in the container; it will be good for a day (or a month if left in the freezer). Whatever she doesn't finish from her plate should be thrown away.

Foods do not need to be hot; room temperature or slightly warm is just fine for most babies. If you need to warm something from the refrigerator, use the microwave with extreme caution—if at all—because of the possibility of uneven temperatures and hot spots within the food that could burn the baby's mouth. Food that is microwaved should be thoroughly stirred so the heat is distributed evenly throughout. If heating food in a baby-food jar, you can place the jar in a pan of warm water for a few minutes.

Don't become a clean-plate fanatic with your baby. When first sampling solids, she will take only small amounts—one or two tablespoons (15 to 30 ml) at a time—and then gradually increase her intake over time. Watch for signs that she is no longer hungry—turning her head, getting fussy, or general disinterest in what you are offering from the spoon. Trying to force her to eat a prescribed amount is not only an exercise in futility but may also set up a bad habit of eating when she has no appetite.

What else do I need to know about feeding my baby?

Do not feed honey to your baby. Infants younger than twelve months of age who eat honey may develop infant botulism, a form of food poisoning that can cause serious damage to the nervous system or very rarely can be fatal.

Keep your baby on breast milk or infant formula (fortified with iron) rather than milk from the dairy case. Infants who drink cow's milk before their first birthday are more likely to develop an allergy to the protein it contains. Cow's milk may also interfere with the absorption of iron contained in other foods.

Steer clear of fruit juices, punch, or other sweetened drinks. Some babies can become so enamored with sweet liquids that they will favor them over more nutritious sources of calories. A good time for your baby to begin enjoying juices is when she can drink them from a cup.

Don't feed your baby foods with added salt or sugar or with spicy flavors. She needs to become accustomed to the basic, unadulterated taste of high-quality foods.

Avoid feeding your baby certain vegetables that you have prepared yourself. Home-prepared spinach, beets, collard greens, turnips, and carrots may contain quantities of nitrates— components of plants and fertilizers—that can be toxic to a young infant. (In addition, well water can contain nitrates in amounts that could be harmful to a baby during the first three months.) Commercial baby-food preparations of these vegetables are made from produce that has been screened for nitrates, and they are safe to use.

Don't let your baby become a grazer. Some parents respond with food (breast, bottle, or snacks) whenever their baby utters any sound remotely suggesting displeasure. The result is nonstop eating by a baby who is never actually hungry or completely satis-fied and who may gain excessive weight.

Remember not to put your baby to bed with a bottle of milk. If she falls asleep with anything other than water in her mouth, bacteria can damage her incoming teeth. A baby who drinks from a bottle while lying flat will also be at greater risk for developing middle-ear infections.

What are some health and safety issues I should be aware of at this age before my child becomes mobile?
Don't leave your baby alone on any elevated surface such as a changing table, kitchen counter, or sofa. He will invariably pick that moment to demonstrate his ability to roll over.

Don't leave your baby unattended even for a few seconds while he is in water, whether bathing in the sink, infant tub, or adult bathtub. He can drown in an inch or two (a few centime-ters) of water.

Everyone in your house, including young children, should know how to dial 911 in case of an emergency. All adults and children over twelve should be trained in infant CPR. Local hospi-tals normally conduct CPR classes on a regular basis.

Be extremely cautious about leaving one of your older chil-dren in charge of your baby, even for a few minutes. This assignment should be considered only for a responsible sibling more than twelve years of age who has been observed handling the baby appropriately for a number of weeks. He or she must have explicit information about your whereabouts, instructions about what to do if the baby cries or has any other type of problem, and names and phone numbers of people to call for help if needed.

Always buckle your baby securely into his car seat, no matter how short the ride. Through the sixth month, he will still be sitting facing backward. (He should not be placed in a forward-facing car seat until he is a year old *and* weighs at least twenty pounds [about 9 kg].) The center of the backseat is the safest location for him. This means that, should he start to fuss, you will have to resist the temptation to turn around and tend to him while your vehicle is in motion. *You should never place your baby in the front passenger seat, especially if your car has a passenger-side air bag.* If the air bag inflates during an accident, it could cause serious or even fatal injuries to a baby.

Never carry your baby while you are also holding a cup of hot liquid. One strong wiggle could result in a scalding injury to one or both of you.

Keep a watchful eye for small objects scattered around your living space. If your baby is going to spend time on the floor, put your face on his level and scan the horizon. Look for stray LEGOS, marbles, action figures, coins, paper clips, pins, pieces of dry pet food, plastic wrappers, electrical cords, or unstable objects that might fall on your baby if given a gentle shove.

Beware of parking your baby in an infant swing or doorway jumper and then turning your attention elsewhere. After four months, a baby with enough wiggle power may be able to squirm out of a swing or even bring the whole thing down.

Keep your baby out of walkers, which are responsible for thousands of accidents every year. These devices will not teach him how to walk or speed up his motor development. Instead, they give your active baby the opportunity to propel himself to the edge of the stairs, investigate whatever is sitting on your coffee table, or flip the walker over when he bumps into an obstruction.

Extremely vigorous play (such as tossing a baby a few inches into the air and catching him) is not a good idea at this age. Rapid accelerations and changes in direction, however playful, can have the same effect as shaking a baby, risking injury to his neck, brain, and eyes.

A baby's skin may become sunburned after as little as fifteen minutes of direct exposure to the sun. Don't allow your baby to have prolonged exposure to direct sunlight (even on a hazy or overcast day), especially between the hours of 10 a.m. and 3 p.m. This is particularly important at higher altitudes or around lakes and seashores, where the sun's ultraviolet light (which provokes the burn) can reflect off sand and water. The use of sunscreen before the age of six months has been controversial because of concerns over the absorption and metabolism of chemicals in these products by young infants.

If you take your baby outdoors for any length of time, keep him in the shade or use an umbrella, and make sure his skin is covered with appropriate clothing (including a hat or bonnet) even if he is in the shade. A small amount of sunscreen may be applied to exposed areas of skin (such as the face, back of the hands, and neck) if for some reason you are in a situation where you cannot provide physical protection from the sun using a hat, clothing, or shade.

Is it time to establish a sleep routine?

Between the fourth and sixth months, your baby will probably have settled into a sleeping routine that is more predictable and easier on everyone during the wee hours. Two naps during the day, one in the morning and one in the afternoon, are a good habit to encourage and maintain. These may last from one to three hours, and at this age you need not awaken your baby from a long nap unless it seems to be interfering with his sleep at night. (Some infants continue to catnap during this period.) Between two and four months or shortly thereafter, your baby should be skipping a night feeding. By six months, he should well be able to handle an eight-hour stretch without being fed unless he was premature or is exceptionally small. But whether this translates into uninterrupted sleep will depend on both your baby and your sleeping arrangements.

If he's down for the night by 8 p.m., he may be genuinely hungry at 4 a.m. But at that hour, unless he's crying with no sign of letting up, you may want to wait a few minutes to see if he might go back to sleep. Delaying his bedtime may help extend his and your uninterrupted sleep in the morning, but a decision to allow him to stay up later must be weighed against other family needs. Ideally, before he is put to bed, there should be some time to wind down with quiet activities—a feeding, some cuddling, some singing, and perhaps a bath. With repetition of a routine, he will begin to associate these particular activities with bedtime and a surrender to sleep. If at all possible, have different people walk through this process with him so he won't come to expect that Mom and Dad are the only people in the world who can bring the day to a close.

Now is a good time to let him learn to fall asleep on his own if he hasn't been doing so already. When he is drowsy but not yet asleep, lay him down, pat him gently, and leave the room. Make sure there's a night-light on so he can see familiar surroundings. If he fusses for more than a few minutes, you can come back for a brief reassurance (perhaps offering some gentle patting on the back) but not a full-blown recap of the nighttime routine. If he persists, let a little more time go by before you return. If there's no end in sight to the crying and you can't stand to let it continue, do whatever works to bring on sleep, and then try again at a later date, perhaps on a weekend night when you have some flexibility in your evening and morning schedules.

If he isn't able to fall asleep by himself by six months of age, the window of opportunity for learning this skill may not be open again for a while. Within the next few months, he is likely to begin demonstrating a normal behavior known as separation anxiety, in which a mighty howl may erupt when you or his closest caregivers are out of his sight, especially at bedtime. As a result, if after six months he's still used to being nursed, held, and rocked until he's sound asleep, you can plan on repeating this ritual for months on end unless you are prepared to endure a vigorous and prolonged protest.

Remember that your baby's nighttime activity may include one or more awakenings that do not necessarily need your attention. If you rush into your baby's room to feed, cuddle, and rock him with every sound he produces, he will become quite accustomed to this first-class room service, and you may find that he is rather reluctant to give it up. Obviously, if he sounds truly miserable and is keeping everyone awake, do whatever is necessary to comfort him and calm things down. At this age it is still better to err on the side of too much attention than too little. After a few more months pass, however, you can become more hard-nosed if he seems intent on having a social hour several times a night.

What can I expect at my child's medical checkups?

If all goes well, your baby will have just two encounters with her health-care provider during these months: a well-baby check at four months and another at six months. During these visits, you'll be asked about your baby's feeding and sleeping patterns, developmental milestones, and signs that she is seeing and hearing well. Be prepared to offer your observations on her head control, use of hands, rolling over, tracking objects with her eyes, responses to sounds, and her other activities. Of course, this is a good time to bring up any questions or concerns about your baby's development.

Your baby's height, weight, and head circumference will be measured and plotted on a growth chart. At the six-month check, it is likely that she will have doubled her birth weight. Unless there are specific reasons to do otherwise, at these visits your baby will normally continue to receive routine immunizations. Be sure to let the health-care provider know if your baby has had an unusual response to any prior immunizations.

CHAPTER 4

SIX TO TWELVE MONTHS

DURING THE SIX MONTHS prior to her first birthday, your baby will begin a momentous transition.

She will want to investigate everything she can get her hands on but will be completely clueless about risks and consequences. And though fervently desiring to explore whatever she can see, she will also be afraid of separation from familiar faces, voices, and hugs. Your challenge will be to protect her—and her environment—while allowing her to stretch her wobbly legs and find out how the world works.

When will my baby start sitting, crawling, and "cruising"?

Between six and nine months, your baby will be figuring out how to sit up and remain steady. First she will need support from pillows or the nearest adult. Then she will begin to prop herself up using her outstretched hands in a "tripod" posture. Eventually she will sit up for minutes at a time without toppling. By nine months, half of all babies are able to maneuver themselves into a sitting position from any other posture. This will give her considerable satisfaction, because her hands will be free to examine interesting objects while she remains upright.

Once your baby discovers the wonders of her world that are visible from a few inches off the floor, she will develop a keen interest in moving herself closer to whatever she spies across the room. Whether she eventually tries to roll, slither, scoot, or crawl toward them, and when she first makes the attempt, will be impossible to predict. If she takes to crawling, her skill will peak between seven and ten months, at which point you will be amazed at the speed with which she can cross the floor. She may use the traditional hands-and-knees approach, scuttle sideways like a crab, or inch forward military-style.

Some babies rarely or never crawl, and crawling doesn't actually appear on standard charts as a developmental milestone. Babies don't need to learn to crawl before they walk, and there is no correlation between this skill and future athletic or intellectual ability. Learning to crawl is not necessary for visual development, hand-eye coordination, or learning to read later in life. If other skills are moving ahead and your baby's doctor confirms that all else is going well, don't panic if she decides to skip crawling and move on to bigger and better things.

At around nine months of age, your baby will make another discovery: Standing upright is really, really fun. Usually someone in the family will pull her to a standing position next to the sofa or a soft chair, and she will gleefully remain there, using her hands to hold her position. Eventually she will figure out how to pull herself to her feet, using any available object that appears tall enough. Next comes the ultimate prewalking thrill of "cruising" from one place to another while holding on to whatever will keep her upright.

If your budding cruiser is going to be turned loose in a room, take a quick visual survey or a brief tour at her level to make certain that she won't find out about the force of gravity the hard way. Particularly important is keeping her off the stairs, which she will find irresistible once she discovers them. After her first birthday, she can begin to learn, with your direct supervision, how to get herself downstairs backward. But until she is clearly "stair safe" many months from now, you will need to consider getting one or more barricades if her activity areas provide potential access to a flight of stairs. These barricades should be the sturdy, horizontal gates with narrow slats (two and three-eighths inches or less apart) or plastic mesh, not the old-fashioned accordion-style, wood-slat barriers, which are less stable and are potential traps for inquisitive heads.

You will also need to choose between pressure-mounted gates, which are easier to install, and hardware-installed gates, which take more effort to attach to a doorway or wall but are more stable. Keep in mind that you should not use pressure-mounted gates at the top of a staircase, because they're easier for a determined child to dislodge.

Letting her suffer some bruising consequences to "teach her a lesson" is a bad idea at this age. Not only will this risk unnecessary injury, but she is in fact not yet capable of understanding and judging the risks involved in her explorations. (She won't start on this learning curve until she is about fifteen months of age.)

When—and how—will my baby start walking?

As your baby continues his relentless efforts to stay upright, he will at some point let go of his favorite support and stand on his own for a few seconds. At the same time or shortly thereafter, he will take a few shaky steps, perhaps with one or both parents cheering him on. Within a week he likely will be purposefully walking from one end of the room to the other, with or without a few unscheduled drops to the floor along the way. His legs will be bent and toes pointed outward, giving a thoroughly precarious appearance to his efforts. But all the lurching and plopping, which you may find nerve-racking to watch, won't slow him down at all.

When will all this ambulating begin? Depending upon his size, center of gravity, genetic code, and temperament, it can begin anywhere between eight and fourteen months of age. If he is on the hefty side, he may have more difficulty hoisting his weight and maintaining his balance. The timing of his first steps has nothing to do with his future batting average or his chances of getting into college, but if he arrives at his first birthday and cannot stand even while being supported, your health-care provider—who will be doing a routine checkup at this age anyway—should be consulted.

What about shoes? Shoes serve little purpose prior to the onset of walking other than to decorate the feet for a family portrait. Once your baby starts to walk routinely, however, you may want to get shoes to protect his feet if he will be walking somewhere—such as in the backyard or a park—where terrain is more likely to contain objects that are unfriendly to little soles.

Shoes should be big enough to allow a half inch of space between his toes and the tip of the shoe, and since his feet will be growing rather rapidly, there is no sense in blowing the family budget on designer footwear. A simple pair of tennis shoes with a sole that grips will suffice. Unless prescribed by a qualified health-care professional to remedy a specific problem, he shouldn't need wedges, heel lifts, or other hardware in his shoes. He won't need arch supports because his arch is covered by a fat pad that will gradually recede over two to three years.

Furthermore, you may notice that while his toes point outward when he walks (because of looseness of the hip ligaments), his feet will tend to point inward (pigeon toes) when he lies down. Both of these situations should straighten out by the time he is about eighteen months old. If any positioning of feet or legs seems extreme or not symmetrical, have your baby's doctor (or, if necessary, an orthopedist who deals with young children) take a look. If you see your baby limp, whether now or in the future, a medical evaluation should be carried out as soon as possible. *Limping is never normal*, and it may in fact be the sign of a significant medical problem.

How will my child use his eyes and hands in new ways?

By seven or eight months of age, your baby's visual capabilities will have matured to the point that she can focus on people and objects across the room, though not quite with the clarity with which she sees things directly in front of her. She may find a mirror entertaining, as she watches the interesting little person who responds exactly to her own movements. She will be more attentive to a variety of colors and shapes and will be rapidly absorbing visual information about the world around her. You will at times notice her staring intently at something across the room. More often she will become fixated on, and apparently fascinated by, some tiny object directly in front of her—a wad of lint, a stray Cheerio, or a little bug.

Her increased visual skills will be matched by new abilities with hands and fingers. By nine months she will have progressed from the mitten or rakelike grasp (using four fingers as a unit against the thumb) to the more precise "pincer" grasp between thumb and one finger. She will also begin cooperative efforts between her two hands to pick up toys, pass an object from hand to hand, or smack two items together to enjoy the sound they produce.

Over the next three months, these investigations with hands will become more sophisticated. She will discover the joy of releasing something from her hands, or actually throwing it, and watching what happens. She will turn an item around and look at it from a variety of angles, rub it, and shake it. If it has a hole, she'll poke a finger into it. If it has parts she can move, she'll push, pull, twist, or spin them. Toward the end of the first year she will enjoy dumping small objects out of a container and then putting them back in, one at a time. She will knock something over and then set it upright, over and over. And, of course, she will bring *everything* directly to her mouth for examination by lips, gums, and tongue.

How will my baby's speech begin to develop?

One of the most pleasant developments between six and twelve months is watching your baby begin to make all sorts of new sounds. After six months he will begin imitating various syllables, primarily with vowels at first. By nine months, gurgling and babbling will be replaced by sounds with consonants such as *baba* or *dada*, either in short bursts or repeated at length. He will probably not assign these sounds to a particular person (for example, *Mama* for his mother) until twelve months or after.

As he progresses toward his first birthday, his "speech" will sound more sophisticated, though without much obvious meaning. Your one-year-old is likely to utilize a vocabulary of a few words, along with some wonderfully modulated babbling that rises and falls with the inflections of real speech. You can almost imagine that he is a visitor speaking a foreign language. He will also begin to communicate with gestures, such as pointing to something he finds interesting, waving bye-bye, or shaking his head to signify no. You may also hear exclamations such as "Uh-oh!"

While his speaking vocabulary may not be extensive at his first birthday, he can understand quite a bit more (in fact, far more than you probably realize) well before that date. After nine months he will begin responding to his own name and may show recognition of familiar people, pets, or objects. He will likely (we hope) respond to the word *no* before he starts using it himself. He may turn his head toward a person or toy you name, and before long he will surprise you by following a simple command.

You can make a major contribution to your child's language

development during these months, even if you're not yet having much conversation. All day long you can name objects that you both see, talk in simple terms about what you are doing, and even look through simple picture books together. Try to keep your vocabulary straightforward and consistent, and don't expose him to hours of convoluted baby talk. Instead, coo and fuss and caress with your voice to your heart's content—using real words.

As cute as you will find his babbling, resist the temptation to repeat back his garbled versions of new words. If he points to a truck and says, "Guck!" be sure to say, "That's right, truck!" rather than leading him to believe that he has truly seen a guck. (One exception: Grandparents almost always proudly assume the names given to them by the first grandchild, such as "Nana and Papa," "Gomba and Bumpa," etc.)

Now is a good time to think about the kinds of sounds your baby will be imitating. Does everyone in the family speak in calm, pleasant tones, or do conversations sound loud and confrontational? Are compliments or complaints exchanged across the kitchen table? Is your baby likely to learn "Shut up!" before he says "I love you"? Is he hearing more words from the adults in his life or from the TV set droning in the corner? If you don't like what your baby is hearing, hold a family meeting and prayer time to help launch some new conversation patterns (and perhaps lower noise levels) at home.

What about "peekaboo" and other games?

In addition to imitating your words and speech patterns, your six- to twelve-month-old will also begin to mimic gestures and movements. You will be pleasantly surprised one day to see him holding his toy telephone to his ear rather than banging it on the floor, or stroking his toy brush across his hair rather than gumming it. By one year of age, he will also enjoy a number of gesture games, such as peekaboo, pat-a-cake, and "so big." ("How big is Tyler?"

Tyler's hands will imitate yours reaching for the sky, as you say, "So-o-o-o big!")

You can have fun with your baby and watch some developmental milestones being reached as he develops his sense of object permanence. At four or five months of age, if something is out of sight, it's also out of mind. If he pushes his rattle off the edge of the sofa, he won't pursue it with his eyes. But at about nine months of age, he can keep an image of something fixed in memory long enough to look for it after it disappears.

Take one of his toys, show it to him, and then hide it under a small cloth. Voilà! He will pull the cloth away to reveal the toy, much to everyone's delight. As he practices this skill, you can try putting two or more obstacles between him and the toy. With the increasing maturity of his sense of object permanence, he will be more persistent in finding it.

What is the next step in feeding my baby solid foods?

During these six months your baby will make another important transition as he becomes nourished primarily by solid foods. If you are just now beginning to offer your baby any food other than milk, you should review pages 67–74, which explain in some detail how to introduce your baby to solids.

We also mentioned some reasons not to begin solids too early (before four months of age), but you don't want to wait too long either. As your baby passes the sixth month, breastfeeding or formula alone will fall short of providing the calories and nutrients he needs. Between six and nine months, he may be more willing to try a variety of foods than after the one-year mark. Thus, your goal at six months will be to begin solids if you haven't by now and then to expand his food horizons gradually and steadily.

By the end of the first year, the general outline of his eating patterns should resemble your own, except for amounts and textures. This raises the question of where you will take your baby nutritionally. If your family's eating habits are chaotic and your diet loaded with fat, salt, and sugar, do you want your baby to reach the same end point? This may be a good time to reevaluate and reconfigure your own food choices.

By nine months you will see some side-to-side chewing movements that signal readiness for foods with a thicker texture. This is a good time to begin trying some mashed or chopped food from the family meal and some finger foods that your baby can feed himself. The latter include items such as small pieces of soft, peeled fruit (peaches or pears, for example), little squares of bread or toast, unsalted crackers, pieces of pancake or soft waffle, and cooked soft pasta.

When first sampling solids he will take only small amounts—one or two tablespoons at a time—and then gradually increase his intake over time. As mentioned in the previous chapter, don't try to make your baby eat everything on his plate. Instead, watch for signs that he is no longer hungry—turning his head, getting fussy, or acting disinterested in what you are offering from the spoon. That's your cut to stop and try again later.

Because of their potential impact on your baby's health, these caveats will be repeated here along with some additional notes for the more experienced solid-food consumer.

- *Do not feed honey to babies under the age of twelve months* because of the risk of infant botulism.

- Keep your baby on breast milk or infant formula (fortified with iron) until he reaches the age of twelve months.

- Keep your baby away from chocolate, peanut butter, shell-fish, egg whites, citrus fruits, strawberries, and tomatoes before his first birthday; these can induce future allergies. Some physicians also add wheat and corn to this off-limits list for the same reason.

- Even more risky to your baby are foods that might cause
  a choking accident. Avoid any foods that are small and
  hard such as seeds, nuts, small candies, uncooked peas,
  and popcorn. Also keep your baby away from foods that
  are sticky, chewy, stringy, or small and round. Peanut butter and hot dogs are thus off-limits, along with grapes,
  uncooked vegetables, raw apples, and dried fruit. In a nut-
  shell, foods that can't be squashed by gums or easily dis-
  solved in saliva or that might fit snugly into a small airway
  don't belong in your baby's mouth.

- Don't feed your baby foods with added salt or sugar, or with
  spicy flavors. He needs to become accustomed to the basic,
  unadulterated taste of high-quality foods.

- Keep up the variety. If your baby seems to ignore everything
  but one or two foods—crackers and bananas, for example—
  don't be frightened or blackmailed into allowing him to
  establish a major food rut. Hold these items and offer him
  a variety of alternatives from the other food groups instead.
  If he refuses, don't panic. When he's hungry, he'll eat what
  you've offered, especially if he hasn't filled his tank with
  milk before mealtime.

- Don't let your baby become a grazer. Some parents respond
  with food (breast, bottle, or snacks) whenever their baby
  utters any sound remotely suggesting displeasure. The
  result is nonstop eating by a baby who is never actually
  hungry or completely satisfied and who might acquire a
  long-term habit of turning to food for comfort. Between six
  and nine months, you can establish mealtime routines:
  breakfast, lunch, and dinner, with midmorning and mid-
  afternoon snacks if you and your baby desire. But when
  meals are over, let them be over.

- Don't put your baby to bed with a bottle of milk or juice. If he falls asleep with anything other than water in his mouth, bacteria can damage his incoming teeth. A baby who drinks from a bottle while lying flat will also be at greater risk for developing middle-ear infections.

- Don't let your baby become a "juiceaholic." Hold off on juices until he can drink them from a cup. Once he has started drinking them on a regular basis, set a four-ounce daily limit, or dilute four ounces with an equal amount of water if you want to offer them more often. Since citrus fruits may provoke allergic responses during the first year, you may want to hold the orange juice until after the first birthday. (Check with your baby's doctor.)

When do I start letting my child feed himself? It's so messy!

Some babies are quite content to let you feed them one spoonful of food after another, while others can't wait to take matters into their own hands (literally) as soon as possible. When your ten-month-old reaches for the feeding spoon, she is primarily interested in it as an object to investigate and manipulate—just like everything else she touches. It is quite unlikely that she will use it to transfer food into her mouth with any consistency until she has passed the fifteen-month mark. Instead, she will probably bang her spoon against the nearest hard object, fling it to the floor, or perhaps dip it into her food—before she bangs and flings it.

Many babies couldn't care less about the spoon, no matter who is holding it, and simply want to turn every solid into a finger food—or an unidentified flying object. Either scenario will serve as an impressive illustration of the word *mess*. After a prolonged mealtime with a self-feeder in this age-group, food may be everywhere—from head to toe on the baby, scattered over a radius of several feet around her high chair, and perhaps decorating a few walls, people, and pets as well.

A balanced approach is for you to manage the spoon with the gooey stuff—the cereal and strained foods—for the first several months, until she is able to handle this assignment herself with a minimum of mess making. You can let her handle a spoon all she wants, of course, without getting food involved. As she passes her first birthday, see if she will imitate you as you show how it's used. At the same time, let her have some of the self-contained finger foods, either before or after spoon feeding. Pay attention, however, to the signs that she isn't hungry: turning her head, not accepting the spoon, getting restless, or tossing foods overboard. If she doesn't want to eat, don't try to feed her, but don't let her play with the food either.

When should I introduce my baby to drinking from a cup?

Another skill you may want your baby to tackle while perched in the high chair is drinking from a cup. This may be a bit easier now than it was a generation or two ago because of the widespread use of spill-proof or sippy cups. These are small plastic cups with tight-fitting lids and a narrow spout through which an infant or toddler can suck or sip his favorite beverage. Bridging the gap between breast or bottle and regular cups used by older children and adults, the sippy cup effectively prevents the child from dumping liquid all over himself and everything around him—unless, of course, the lid isn't attached snugly.

Many children use these until the preschool years, by which time improved coordination enables them to drink from the genuine article with less chance of a spill. On the other hand, some have raised concerns that using sippy cups long after a child can master an open cup may lead to some temporary difficulties with clarity of speech. Also, taking a sippy cup with milk or juice to bed could promote tooth decay, as does a bedtime bottle.[7]

If you are adventurous, you can always go straight to the open cup. Since this involves hand control, new swallowing skills, and liquid that might go anywhere and everywhere, take your time. The cup you choose for your baby may be easier to use if it has two handles or, depending on his preference, no handles. A weighted bottom will help keep it oriented topside up, and sturdy construction is a must.

After your baby's gotten the hang of taking food from a spoon, you can try putting a little water in his cup. When you first put it to his lips, he will probably not know what to do. After you let a few drops enter his mouth, he may swallow, let it run down his chin, or some of each. Be patient. Only one in four babies will master the skill of drinking from a cup by the age of nine months, and it may be an additional six months before most of the liquid goes where it belongs.

How can I avoid high-chair hazards?

As your baby begins to spend more time with solids each day, you may find it easier to feed her in a high chair. As with all baby equipment, a few simple precautions will help prevent unpleasant or even serious accidents.

- As with bathtubs and car seats, rule number one with high chairs is *never leave your baby unattended while she is sitting in it*.

- Make certain that the chair has a broad base so it cannot be easily tipped over. If you use a chair that folds, make sure it is locked into place before your baby gets in.

- Take the few extra seconds to secure your baby with the chair's safety straps. This will prevent her from wiggling and sliding out of position or standing up to survey the horizon, both of which could result in a serious injury.

- Before your baby is seated, make sure the chair is at a safe distance from the nearest wall or counter. Otherwise, a healthy shove from your young diner might topple her and the chair to the floor.

- Don't let other children play under or climb on the high chair.

- Clean food debris off the chair and tray after each meal. Your baby may have no reservations about sampling any leftovers—in various states of decay—that are within finger range.

If you use a portable baby seat that clamps onto a table when you travel or eat out, observe a few additional precautions:

- Make sure the table is steady enough to support both chair and baby and that the chair is securely clamped to the table before your baby gets in. Card tables, glass tops, tables supported only by a center post, and extension leaves are not strong or stable enough for this job.

- Position the chair so your baby can't push against one of the table legs and literally "shove off" for a voyage to the floor.

- The chair should attach to the bare surface of the table, not a tablecloth or place mat that can slide off.

- Don't let older children play under the table or seat, since they might accidentally bump and dislodge it.

What else should I do to "baby-proof" my home?
Take a child's-eye tour of whatever living space will be available to your crawler/cruiser/walker. Are there any top-heavy items—chairs, tables, floor lamps, bookshelves—that might fall if pulled by your baby? Are any electrical cords or outlets within

reach? (Install plastic plugs to block unused outlets from inquisitive fingers.) Do you see any wires with frayed insulation? These are a hazard to everyone, not just the baby. What about cords dangling down from a curling or steam iron resting on a counter or ironing board? A yank on one of these could cause not only a hazardous bonk on her head or body but also a very painful burn.

Are there any small objects lying around that, upon entering her mouth, might end up in her airway? Your vigilance regarding small objects will be a daily concern if you have older children at home, because their toys and games tend to have lots of tiny parts and pieces that have a way of dispersing throughout your home. How about cords attached to draperies and blinds? These should be looped or tied on a hook well out of reach to prevent the baby from getting tangled in them.

Don't leave your prized china or other valuable breakables within reach of a newly mobile baby and then demand that she not touch them. She will have no concept of the difference between a cup made by Wedgwood and one brought home from Wendy's, except, perhaps, by the distinctive sounds they make when they hit the floor. Your expensive collectibles should be displayed (or stored) out of reach during this season of your child's life.

While some recommend that your kitchen be kept off-limits to little explorers, this will probably not be a realistic option. Most parents and older children traverse the kitchen many times each day, and dealing with a barricade every time is a major nuisance. Lots of family interactions take place in kitchens, and your baby will not want to be left out.

This will mean, however, relocating cleaning compounds and other chemicals to higher ground. Bleach, furniture polish, and drain cleaners are particularly hazardous, and automatic-dishwasher powder can be extremely irritating if it gets into the mouth. Sharp objects, which of course are abundant in kitchens, must also be kept out of reach at all times. If you have an automatic dishwasher, be sure to keep the door latched when you are not loading or unloading it. A wide-open dishwasher door is not only an irresistible climbing spot but also a gateway to all sorts of glassware and sharp utensils.

Many families set aside a low cupboard for "baby's kitchen stuff"—a collection of old plastic bowls, cups, spoons, lids, and other safe unbreakables that she can examine and manipulate to her heart's content. (By the way, she will probably spend a fair amount of time moving the cupboard door back and forth on its hinge.) You may want to steer her toward this particular cupboard and away from the others (this will take lots of repetition) or make the arrangement more formal by installing plastic safety latches in the cupboards and drawers that are off-limits.

While kitchens are difficult to barricade, bathrooms are another story. Like kitchens, they are full of potential hazards: medications, cleaners, and, most important, bodies of water. Any medications (prescription or over-the-counter, including vitamins and iron) and cleaning substances must be stored well out of reach and returned to their secure spot *immediately* after each use.

Never leave a baby unattended in the bath, even at this age, and be certain to empty the tub as soon as you're done with it. Open toilets are an irresistible destination for a cruiser. The possible consequences of a baby's investigation of an unflushed toilet are both unsafe and stomach turning. More important is the possibility that a top-heavy toddler might lean over far enough to fall in.

Never leave hair dryers, curlers, or other electrical devices plugged in after you use them. For that matter, no one should be using any of these items when the baby (or anyone else) is in the bathtub, unless you have a very large bathroom with a lengthy distance between appliance and water. If your baby or an older child tries to take the hair dryer for a swim, *even if it's turned off but plugged in*, the resulting shock could be lethal.

Unlike most kitchens, bathrooms have doors that can be shut to prevent unsupervised entry. If an enterprising explorer learns to turn door handles, an additional high latch may need to be installed.

Survey your home for "what's hot and what's not." Radiators, heaters, floor furnace grills, and fireplace screens can all become surprisingly hot, and a protective barrier between these surfaces and little fingers will be needed, at least during some times of the year.

Be sure the handles of pots on hot burners don't extend over the edge of the stove, since one healthy pull could result in a severely scalded child. Some stoves also have exposed knobs that babies and toddlers might love to twist and turn. If these are easily detachable, you may want to remove them between meals. You can also buy safety covers at a hardware store.

A similar reminder applies to hot liquids such as soups and gravies near the edge of your dining table, especially if they sit on a tablecloth that could be pulled from below. Avoid carrying your wiggly explorer and a cup of hot coffee or tea at the same time. One sudden twist on her part could fling hot liquid over both of you.

Set your water heater temperature below 120°F (49°C) to minimize the risk of an accidental scald from the tap.

How about those houseplants? Now is the time to move houseplants out of reach, unless you know for certain that they are nontoxic and you don't care if they get mangled sometime during the next few months. Otherwise, your child might choose to sample the leaves and stems, which may irritate the lining of the mouth or even be overtly toxic. In order to prevent your explorer from having a close encounter with the dirt around any plants that remain at floor level, you can cover the soil with screen mesh.

Finally, think about your baby's introduction to the great outdoors. When the weather's nice and the family gathers in the backyard, what interesting but hazardous items might cross her path? Once again, make a baby's-eye survey of any area that she might reach (if she's a skilled crawler, keep in mind how fast she can move while your attention is diverted).

If you have a swimming pool, make sure that a childproof fence—at least four feet high, not climbable, and equipped with a self-closing and self-latching gate—surrounds it. (Some states require this safety barrier by law.) If your yard contains a spa, it should be securely covered when not in use. Pool and hot-tub drain covers should be checked periodically to make sure they are properly in place. If not, a child's hand or even hair could be pulled into the outlet by the suction created by the pump, and she might be unable to break free. Children have drowned in such circumstances. As a backup precaution, make sure that the pump's on-off switch is readily accessible.

Check the lawn for mushrooms, and if you are not absolutely certain they are nontoxic, get rid of them, because anything your baby finds at this age is likely to go straight into her mouth. Are there any garden tools, insecticides, fertilizers, or other unfriendly items lying around? The more potential dangers you can eliminate from her immediate access, the more you can enjoy your time outdoors with her.

One other outdoor hazard you must not ignore is the sun. A baby's skin is very sensitive to the ultraviolet (UV) light generated by the sun, and at peak times of the day as little as fifteen minutes of direct exposure can provoke an unpleasant burn. (This is a particular problem at higher altitudes and around lakes and oceans.) But sunburns can also occur on hazy or overcast days because UV light penetrates both haze and cloud cover.

If your baby is going to be experiencing the great outdoors for any length of time, try to avoid the 10 a.m. to 3 p.m. time of peak intensity, keep her in the shade as much as possible, and utilize appropriate clothing (as well as a hat or bonnet) for protection. An explorer who is going to be in and out of sunlight will benefit from a sunscreen with a sun protection factor (SPF) rating of at least 15, applied an hour before she ventures forth. If you are going to take her with you into the pool, use a waterproof version and reapply it after you are done. Occasionally a baby will react to the UV-protecting ingredient known as PABA, so you may want to avoid sunscreens containing this compound. If your baby has very sensitive skin, you might take your sunscreen for a "test drive" by applying some to a small area of her skin (an inch or a couple of centimeters wide) for several hours to see if any reaction develops.

You may want to consider using insect repellent for your child (and yourself) if you're going to be outside for any length of time—especially between dusk and dawn, when mosquitoes (including those that carry West Nile virus) are more likely to be biting. This is particularly important if there are reports of mosquito-transmitted disease in your area.

DEET (N,N-diethyl-m-toluamide) is widely used as an active ingredient in insect repellents and is considered safe for use in children over two months of age.[8] According to the Food and Drug Administration (FDA), products containing another active ingredient, oil of eucalyptus, are not recommended for children younger than three years old.[9]

Equally (if not more) important for safety is proper use of repellents:

- When applying repellent, put it on your hands first and then rub it on the child's skin, avoiding the eyes, mouth, and any cuts or irritated skin.

- Don't apply repellent to a child's hands (which often go into their mouths).

- Sunscreen and insect repellent can be applied at the same time (put on the sunscreen first), but products containing both should be avoided. To be effective, sunscreen usually has to be applied more often than repellent.

- When the outdoor activities are over for the day, wash the skin on which the repellent was applied.

Remember that clothing with long pants and long sleeves, weather permitting, can serve as a physical barrier to bites by insects and other critters (such as ticks).

What else do I need to know about keeping my baby safe?

Perpetual vigilance is the price of child rearing, at least for now. You must develop an ongoing sense of your child's whereabouts, a third eye and ear that are tuned in to him, even when he is in a confined and seemingly safe space such as his crib.

The riskiest times will be those when you are distracted, frazzled, or just plain weary. You may be in the middle of a project involving hazardous tools or materials—a long overdue deep cleaning, for example. Suddenly the phone rings, or someone is at the door, or another child cries out in another room. Before you drop everything to attend to the new situation, look at what might be open, exposed, or available to your baby. Could he get to any of it? You may have to delay your response for a few moments while you ensure there is no way your baby in motion can get his hands on something dangerous.

Beware of those times in the day—especially the late afternoon—when your energy may be low, your mind preoccupied, and your patience short. One or more other children may be irritable at this time, competing for your attention. But don't lose track of your youngest crawler/cruiser/toddler, who may have just discovered something interesting that was dropped under the kitchen table.

Sometime in your parenting career, you may reach a point of such sheer exhaustion that you just have to lie down for a little while. Do you let an older child watch the baby or let him roam around your bedroom while you close your eyes for a few precious minutes? Think hard before you stretch your safety boundaries. Some cautions about using older children as babysitters were brought up in the previous chapter, but you must be even more wary when you have a new explorer. An older child is more likely to become distracted by a friend or toy, and a major problem could develop during a few moments of inattention. If you are really that tired, see if a trusted adult such as a friend, neighbor, or relative might relieve you for one or more hours' respite.

How early should I begin disciplining my child?

Considering developmental milestones, you can't expect a baby under eight months of age to follow directions, although certain behaviors (such as day and night sleeping patterns) may be shaped by parents. As your baby becomes mobile, you will need to begin establishing and enforcing limits through a variety of approaches. If you haven't started some basic molding and training of your child by eighteen months, you'll be off to a late start.

Why does my baby have anxiety around other people at this age?

As early as six months of age, but usually between eight to twelve months, your baby, who may have seemed so comfortable around everyone, will begin showing anxiety among unfamiliar people. The approach of someone new or someone she hasn't seen for a while will provoke a wide-eyed stare, usually followed by wailing and clinging to you for protection. This is called stranger anxiety.

The flip side of stranger anxiety is separation anxiety, an increased unwillingness to be separated from the main caregiver—usually (but not always) Mom. Your baby may begin to cry when you simply step into another room for a moment or put her into her crib for a nap. If and when she's about to be left with a relative or a sitter, the crying may escalate into a wailing and clinging session of spectacular proportions.

Separation issues can turn into an emotional upheaval for parents and baby alike. On one hand, it's nice to know that your child thinks so highly of you, so to speak. But having your baby cling to you like superglue, hearing a prolonged chorus of protest every night at bedtime, or wondering whether you'll ever have a night (or weekend) away without massive guilt can begin to feel like a ball and chain.

Your approach to this development should be, first of all, to avoid extremes. Some parents, especially with the first baby, feel that their supreme calling in life is to prevent their child from experiencing one minute of unhappiness. Whatever it takes to prevent crying they will do, and whatever the baby seems to want they will provide, immediately and without question. But this is an exercise in futility and a setup for creating an over-indulged, selfish, and miserable child. Conversely, parents who take a very controlling approach to child rearing may not be very concerned about separation anxiety. But they also run the risk of being inattentive and neglectful of a young child's emotions in general. Both approaches stake out a path of least resistance that may seem to work for now but may also exact a terrible price in the future.

Since you are no doubt sensitive to your child's emotions but probably don't want to feel entirely controlled by her cries and moods, you'll be relieved to know that separation anxiety is a normal phase of development. It's virtually inevitable, but you can buffer its impact. For example, if a sitter is coming to your home, have her arrive a half hour early so she can get acquainted with your baby in an unhurried manner. If you are dropping the baby off at a place that is new to her, try to stick around for a while to allow your baby time to explore and get accustomed to the new environment. When it's time for you to depart, don't stoke the emotional fires with a hand-wringing send-off. Let your baby get involved in an activity with the caregiver, say a short and sweet good-bye, and then leave. (If your baby or toddler is going to spend time with a favorite set of grandparents or an aunt and uncle whom she knows well, you may find that your departure barely provokes any response at all.)

The separation process will be much more unpleasant if your baby is tired or hungry. If you can schedule your departure after a nap or a meal, it may go more smoothly. There is no harm in finding a so-called transitional object, such as a soft toy or small blanket, to serve as a comforting reminder of things that are familiar to her. Once this object has been picked out by your child, you may want to buy a duplicate (or in the case of a blanket, cut it in half) to have on hand if the original is lost or in the washer. Tattered, stained, and probably a little smelly, this item may become a treasured souvenir of your child's early years.

Why is my baby fighting bedtime now?

For some babies, separation becomes a major issue at bedtime. If your baby isn't used to falling asleep on her own by eight or nine months of age, you may be in for some stormy nights ahead if you try to revise her routine. If she wakes up during the night, not only will she sound off, but she may also pull herself to a stand in her crib and rattle it vigorously until you tend to her. (Make sure you have adjusted the mattress and side rails of the crib so she can't tumble out.) Even a baby who originally was doing very well at bedtime may start resisting the process, crying and clinging to you when it's time to go to sleep.

You can still work toward bringing her into a state of drowsiness (but not quite asleep) using a little nursing or formula, rocking and singing, augmented perhaps by her favorite soft object.

Then lay her down, pat her gently, reassure her, say good night, and leave. The same approach should be used if she begins awakening during the night. If this is a new behavior for her, check to be sure she isn't ill, grossly wet or soiled, or tangled in her blanket. Tend to these concerns if needed, but keep your visit quick, quiet, and businesslike and then say good night. She shouldn't need any middle-of-the-night feedings at this point; if you continue offering them well after the six-month mark, you'll only be providing room service and bleary-eyed companionship, not meeting any nutritional needs.

Obviously, if interrupted sleep doesn't bother anyone, you may choose to leave things alone. Eventually your child will sleep through the night on her own—though with some children it may take many more months before this occurs spontaneously. But if you have an infant older than nine months who is still routinely rousing everyone from sleep two or three times a night, even after you have been providing a boring response for weeks, you may want to take more deliberate measures to bring this behavior to a close.

One approach would involve picking a time—usually on a weekend—when you say good night and then resolve not to return until the next morning, no matter how often (or how long) the crying goes on. Obviously, you would not want to try this "commando" approach with a child who is sick, or on a hot summer night when the windows are open, or when you need to be wide-awake the next day, or (most important) if *both* parents are not wholeheartedly ready for it. If you try this tactic, you should greet your baby in the morning with smiles, hugs, and reassurance. Normally after three, or at most, four nights (if not fewer), she will get the picture and sleep through the night thereafter. If you take this approach, using a video monitor may give you some peace of mind and allow you to intervene in the event of a safety problem.

What can I expect during medical checkups at this age?

During this six-month period your baby will not need as many routine checkups as he did during the first six months. Normally, visits are carried out at six months, nine months, and one year of age. Your baby's doctor will, as before, measure progress in height, weight, and head circumference. A review of developmental milestones and a check from head to toe will also be on the agenda. You should feel free to ask questions about feeding or behavior problems that might concern you, and check for any specific guidelines about the introduction of solid foods. You can expect some input about safety at home as well, including directions about appropriate action to take in case your baby accidentally swallows a toxic substance or an overdose of medication.

Immunizations that protect your baby against dangerous illnesses—diphtheria, tetanus, whooping cough (pertussis), polio, rotavirus infection, hepatitis B—and aggressive bacteria—*Haemophilus influenzae* type B and pneumococci—will be continued during these visits. After your baby arrives at the six-month mark, his doctor will also offer a yearly vaccine against influenza, which is now recommended for all infants and children six months and older.

If for any reason your baby has fallen behind on his basic immunization schedule, talk to the doctor about a timetable for catching up. Now that he has reached the six-month mark, you may be tempted to slack off on vaccinations, especially if your budget is tight. But you should press on and complete this process because the illnesses that you may prevent can be devastating. If you are short on funds, check with your local health department about the availability of low-cost immunizations.

Between the ninth and twelfth months, your baby may be given a skin test to detect contact with the bacteria that causes tuberculosis (*Mycobacterium tuberculosis*). This test is usually *not* done unless there is reasonable concern that your child may have been exposed to this organism. By the one-year checkup your baby may have blood drawn to check for anemia (a shortage of red blood cells) or exposure to lead. If anemia is present at this age, it usually indicates a need for more iron in the baby's diet. Your doctor will give you specific recommendations if this is the case.

While it may seem a little early to be taking your baby to the dentist, the American Academy of Pediatric Dentists recommends a dental check once the first teeth come in, and no later than the first birthday.

CHAPTER 5

TWELVE TO TWENTY-FOUR MONTHS

DURING THESE NEXT several months—which will pass more quickly than you might imagine—you will enter into some crucial interactions with your child. By the end of this year he needs to know and understand that you love him fervently and unconditionally and, at the same time, that you are in charge and he isn't. *If either or both of these messages are not clearly established by the second birthday (or within the few months that follow), your child-rearing tasks during the following years are likely to be far more difficult.* His patterns of relating to you and any other people close to him, whether generally pleasant or continually combative, are likely to become more firmly entrenched by the third birthday and may continue for years thereafter.

You don't need to do everything perfectly this year to bring up a healthy, delightful child, however. An isolated mistake or even getting on the wrong track for a number of weeks isn't going to ruin his life. God has granted parents a good deal of time on the learning curve and given children a great deal of resiliency. So take a deep breath, fasten your seat belt, stay on your knees (not just when you're picking up toys), and amid all the challenges, don't forget to step back once in a while to marvel at this little person you are nurturing.

What developments should I expect in height, weight, and other physical features?

If you haven't already done so during one of your child's well-baby checkups, take a look at the growth curve that should be in her medical chart. Better yet, ask the doctor or office staff for a copy that you can continue updating on your own. You'll notice that the average rate of growth during the second year is slower than it was during the first twelve months. A normal one-year-old will have tripled his birth weight but then will gain only three to five more pounds (about 1.4 to 2.3 kg) by age two. Similarly, regardless of gender, your child will add roughly four inches (a little over 10 cm) of height between the first and second birthdays, less than half the height gained during the first year. Interestingly, while your child's head will increase in circumference only about an inch (2.5 cm) over the next twelve months, by age two it will have reached 90 percent of its adult size.

The percentile curves shown on the growth charts begin to diverge more noticeably after the first twelve months. In other words, the differences in height and weight between a child who is at the 90th percentile (that is, larger than 90 percent of the children his age) and one of the same age who is at the 10th percentile will become more dramatic after the first birthday. For most children, position on the growth chart depends largely on genetics, with a height and weight trajectory that will be fairly predictable after the first eighteen to twenty-four months of life have been tracked, barring an unusual problem or chronic illness. If your child is "falling off" a curve—that is, she has been at a certain percentile of weight and height for a number of months and then appears to shift to a significantly lower level during subsequent checkups—a medical or nutritional problem may be present, and your health-care provider may recommend further evaluation.

Even though she will not be experiencing drastic changes in height and weight, the baby look will begin to fade away between her first and second birthdays. With more muscle motion, her arms and legs will look longer and leaner and her abdomen less prominent. Her face will gradually shift from the round, nonspecific but universally appealing look of a baby to more well-defined features that will give you a preview of her future appearance. As you watch her enthusiastically attempting to blow out two birthday candles, don't be surprised if you find yourself wondering, *Where did my baby go?*

The debut of walking may already have occurred two or three months before the first birthday, or it may be a few months away. By eighteen months, your child should have this skill down pat. While early starters won't have any long-term advantage over the late bloomers who are otherwise normal, they will be somewhat ahead of the game in maturity of their gait. It takes a few months to progress from the broad-based, lurching, hands-up, toes-out, frequent-faller toddling walk to a smoother, more narrow-based gait with fewer falls, improved maneuvering, and—a big thrill for many kids—the ability to use hands to carry things while on the move.

Parents watching a toddler career around the room may wonder about the alignment of the legs: Are they turned outward too far? Does one foot point in a different direction from the other? During the first several weeks of walking, this may be impossible to answer. If you see an obvious, consistent difference in the orientation of the legs, however, you should have your toddler's health-care provider watch her move up and down the office corridor.

He or she may want an opinion from an orthopedist to determine whether specific intervention is in order.

The vast majority of toddler gait concerns resolve on their own as weeks pass and coordination improves. However, an obvious limp or a toddler's sudden unwillingness to walk after she clearly knows how is always abnormal and should be evaluated medically as soon as possible.

What developments should I expect in vision, hearing, and language?

The average one-year-old can see well enough to spy small objects across the room or planes flying overhead. By the age of two he will probably approach normal vision, although it is difficult to measure accurately at this age. If he seems to be squinting a lot or bringing objects right up to his face before he interacts with them or doesn't seem to be tracking objects with his eyes, an exam by an ophthalmologist (a physician who specializes in eye problems) would be a good idea. An exam is also needed if you see obvious crossing of his eyes (even temporarily) or if they don't seem to be moving in the same direction. Ideally, you'll consult a pediatric ophthalmologist, a physician specializing in children's eye problems, although many ophthalmologists deal with all age-groups. Unless specially trained and equipped, your primary-care physician will not be able to determine the visual acuity of a one-year-old.

While major visual problems are uncommon in one-year-olds, hearing can become impaired if ear infections and colds—which are not at all unusual in this age-group—leave persistent thick fluid behind one or both eardrums. If the problem persists untreated for weeks or months, your child's ability to understand and generate language can be delayed.

You should consider the possibility of a hearing problem in your toddler if:

- He doesn't turn in response to sounds or ignores you when you call him.

- He isn't using any single words (such as *Mama*) by the age of twelve to fifteen months, or his speech is unintelligible by the age of two.

- His responses to sounds seem to be selective. He may actually be hearing low-pitched sounds better than high-pitched ones, or one ear may be affected but not the other.

If you have any concerns about hearing loss, by all means have his ears and hearing checked—the sooner the better. While your health-care provider can usually determine whether there is fluid behind the eardrum or identify other physical problems, a detailed assessment of hearing in this age-group requires special training and equipment. A safe and painless test with the intimidating name "brainstem auditory evoked response" (also called "auditory evoked potentials") can test hearing without your child's cooperation, but you may have to travel some distance to have it done. If your toddler's physician recommends this test or a consultation with an ear, nose, and throat (ENT) specialist, don't hesitate to do so.

Assuming that hearing is normal, your child will probably have a speaking vocabulary of a few words at his first birthday and about ten times that many at his second, some of which he may combine into two- or three-word sentences. What he can *understand*, however, will become much more impressive as the year progresses. As he moves past the eighteen-month mark, he will point to all sorts of things—people, objects, body parts—when asked about them ("Where is your nose?" "Where's Auntie Linda?"). By the second birthday, the unintelligible strings of sounds that sounded like a foreign language at the beginning of the year will be honed down to simple statements or even questions. Even more amazing is seeing your walking baby, who not long ago lay helpless in a crib, following a simple command such as "Go get the ball."

Over the next several months, you will have the unique and important opportunity to help expand your child's language skills. You won't need a teaching credential, a master's degree, or special training in child development to do this. Instead, you will simply need to "be there" when you are with him. Keep your antennae up and be ready to give him dozens of little doses of your attention and conversation throughout the day.

How can I encourage my child's language development?

You can take the following steps to model and encourage this skill:

Take advantage of his curiosity. When your child approaches you with an object or points to something and makes a sound (which may rise at the end like a question—"Car?"), you've got his attention. Name the object and say something simple about it ("Yes, that's Daddy's car"). He doesn't need a lecture about auto mechanics, of course, but don't be afraid to aim your comment a little beyond what you think he might understand.

Talk to him while you're doing everyday chores. Folding clothes may be boring to you, but if he's watching, it doesn't take any extra time to name the items or say what you're doing with them.

Read to him. Reading simple stories to your child, especially at bedtime, is an extremely worthwhile activity to begin this year, if you haven't already. (Be sure to let him see what you are reading and to identify for him anything he finds interesting in the pictures.) His interest and understanding will increase dramatically over the course of the year. By age two, in fact, he may be able to fill in the blanks in a story he knows well, anticipating and saying one or more words at favorite spots along the way.

Remember to speak to your child using clear, meaningful words. Use a pleasant tone of voice, but avoid baby talk, and don't repeat his unique mispronunciations of words, even if they *are* cute.

Don't make reading to him an issue if he's not interested at the particular story time you have in mind. Usually you won't meet much resistance to looking at books at bedtime, but your child may not be as interested during daylight hours.

Don't rely on "educational" videos to build your toddler's language skills. They may be pleasant diversions, but you shouldn't hand the responsibility of your child's language development over to impersonal curriculum or entertainers. Live humans who are paying attention to *him* are much more effective.

How can I help my toddler explore her world?

This year your toddler will continue to explore whatever she finds around her. Her ability to pick up and manipulate objects both large and small will become much more refined and coordinated during the coming months. By her second birthday, she will enjoy scribbling with crayons (preferably not on the walls), stacking four or five items and then knocking them over, playing with clay, and sticking pegs of various shapes into similarly shaped holes. Many toddlers also become fascinated with things that go around. Wheels that spin on toy cars, pedals on bicycles, a lazy Susan you don't need anymore, or a saucepan lid turned upside down on the kitchen floor may become objects of your child's greatest affection.

Between eighteen and twenty-four months of age, most toddlers also become enamored with balls; holding, rolling, tossing, watching them bounce around, and then chasing them hold endless interest and delight. Beware, however, of small round objects (such as marbles) that might be put in the mouth and then accidentally inhaled. Best bet: Buy your toddler her own inexpensive inflatable twelve- to eighteen-inch beach ball. It's quiet, it can't do much damage, she can carry it around when she doesn't want to throw it, and it's easy to replace.

By her second birthday, you may get a preview of your child's preference for using the right or left hand. But she may also use the spoon with her right, scribble with her left, and throw a ball with either. Don't try to push the use of one hand over the other, and don't worry about speeding up the process. She'll sort out her handedness in due time.

This year your child will significantly increase her grasp of the way things work. Her sense of object permanence—the idea that something is still present even if she can't see it—will become more sophisticated. Not only will she learn to search for a toy she saw you place under two or three blankets or pillows, but she will also become a whiz at little hide-and-seek activities. If she sees you stick a toy in your pocket, she won't forget where it went. (Don't try to fake her out with some sleight of hand, however. "Magic tricks" where items appear or disappear unexpectedly will confuse the toddler's budding sense of object permanence.)

Brief episodes of playacting and imitation will become more sophisticated over the course of the year. Watch her hold the toy phone to her ear (or yours), try to brush her hair, rock her baby, or turn the steering wheel on a toy car. As the months pass, she will try to engage you in some of these scenarios. If you can stop for a few moments to pretend to drink out of the toy cup she offers you or talk on her phone, you'll make her day. Finding the right balance between responding to these overtures often enough to satisfy your child but without endless interruption to whatever you're trying to get done is an art in parenting.

How can I avoid "toddler-care burnout"?

During the second twelve months, your child will display a gamut of behaviors and emotions that, depending on your frame of mind, you may find confusing, amusing, or downright exasperating. A little preparation and some insight into the emerging worldview of the one-year-old can help you sort out and manage this important developmental passage.

First and foremost, keep in mind that above all else your toddler needs to know that she is loved, accepted, and "at home" with you and that you are on her side without reservation—even when you won't give her everything she wants. She needs kind and loving words and actions all day long, and she will come to you frequently for them.

Expect overtures of all sorts, often with arms outstretched, many times during the day as your toddler seeks

- cuddles and hugs;

- comfort after a bump or bruise;

- reassurance after being frightened;

- help with a problem, such as getting something out of reach or fixing a misbehaving toy;

- your enthusiastic reaction to something she has brought you;

- your response to a simple question (or sounds that resemble a question);

- relief from being hungry, thirsty, or having a wet or dirty diaper;

- invitations to role-play (at her direction)—pretending to talk on her toy phone, for example; and

- confirmation that you are still "there" when she has not seen you for a few minutes.

These approaches for comfort, input, and help will not last forever, and to the best of your ability they shouldn't be ignored. For a toddler they provide some critical fact-finding about how things work, how to get help, and who cares about her. They probably will also have a major impact on the way she interacts with the world at large in subsequent years. In a very real sense, you are her launching pad, and after determining that her base of operations is safe and secure, she will be able to explore an expanding world around her.

You may find it difficult or impossible to stop whatever you're doing and respond immediately every time your toddler comes or calls to you. In fact, a little wait at times won't hurt: She needs to learn that she is important, but not Queen of the Domain. If you're on the phone or up to your elbows in dishwater, it's quite all right to acknowledge one of her overtures with "I hear you, and I'll help you in a few minutes."

As with everything else in parenting, extremes are best avoided. If your toddler is clinging to you every minute of the day or whining and crying if you pay attention to anything or anyone else, she may be too attached to you and not spending enough of her day exploring and learning about other parts of the known universe. In this case, you may need to be more assertive about delaying your response to her when you need to tend to other business. On the other hand, if you find yourself issuing a steady stream of brush-offs, uh-huhs, or irritated sighs ("What is it now?!"), take a few minutes to review your own state of mind or think about some ways to recharge your batteries.

How do I start establishing healthy eating patterns?

By her first birthday, your toddler should have a working knowledge of a variety of foods from the well-known groups in addition to her milk. Remember that while cow's milk may be introduced after the first birthday if your child doesn't demonstrate any allergy to it, *whole* milk—not low-fat or nonfat—should be on the menu. Cholesterol is not an issue at this age, and the fat in whole milk is useful in building a number of tissues, including the central nervous system. Beware, however, of allowing a budding milkaholic to push her milk consumption past sixteen to twenty-four ounces (one to one and one-half pints) per day. Not only will this curb her interest in other types of food, but large amounts of milk may also interfere with the absorption of iron from other foods, which in turn can lead to anemia (a deficiency in red blood cells).

During this year you will want to establish a routine with meals and snacks, if you haven't already. Three meals and two small snacks at generally consistent times are far preferable to nonstop grazing, which trains a child to eat for all kinds of reasons other than hunger, scatters food everywhere, and may lead to a choking accident if a toddler stumbles with food in her mouth. This is a good time to establish a routine of sitting down at the table before eating, which actually is beneficial for adults and older children as well.

A fair amount of the food she eats at a meal can consist of small portions of whatever the rest of the family is having, as long as it

- isn't too hot in temperature;

- isn't too hot in seasoning, overly salty or sweet, or swimming in butter or grease;

- is either mushy or cut into small, easily chewed pieces. Continue to avoid foods that could easily lodge in the airway.

One development on the food front that catches many parents off guard is the erratic appetite of the toddler. She may eat voraciously one day and show little interest in food the next, or consume a sizable breakfast and then quit after only a few bites of the day's other meals. With her nonstop activity during waking hours, this apparent inconsistency in fueling patterns may not make sense, but it is not uncommon. Also remember that growth is not as rapid now as it was during the first year, and that the average toddler needs only about one thousand calories a day—not a huge amount of food—to meet her nutritional needs.

Your goal should be to offer her a variety of foods in modest amounts each day. If she turns you down, don't turn your mealtime into a battle zone. Attempting to force a toddler to eat anything is an exercise in futility, and insisting that she can't leave the table or have another meal until she has finished every last speck of her vegetables will lead to miserable, exhausting times around the dinner table. You'll also need to decide how much mess you can tolerate. Some postmeal cleanup will be necessary while your child learns the fine points of hand-spoon-mouth coordination, but you shouldn't confuse the pitching of food and fluids in all directions with her self-feeding learning curve. One way to minimize the mess is to keep serving sizes small.

Don't panic and then offer your toddler something she really likes out of fear that she won't get enough to eat. This may turn into a subtle form of dietary extortion and is a surefire way to create long-term food habits that may be nutritionally inadequate. If she doesn't want much now, put the plate back in the fridge and warm it up for the next meal. When she's hungry, she'll eat. If you are worried about her food intake, write down what she has eaten over a week's time and run it by her doctor. If she is active, showing developmental progress, and gaining on the growth chart, she's getting enough. Remember: No normal child will voluntarily starve herself.

The listing that follows will give you a rough idea of the types of foods and quantities that are appropriate for this age-group. Remember, however, that your toddler may eat less or more than these amounts on any given day.

- Breads, cereals, and other grains: four to six servings per day
  One serving = 1/4 to 1/3 cup cereal; 1/4 cup pasta or rice; 1/4 to 1/2 slice bread or bagel

- Milk/dairy products: two to three servings per day
  One serving = 1/2 cup milk; 1/2 to 1 ounce cheese; 1/3 to 1/2 cup yogurt or cottage cheese

- Vegetables: two to three servings per day
  One serving = 1 or 2 tablespoons

- Fruit: two to three servings per day
  One serving = 1/4 cup cooked or canned; 1/2 piece fresh; 1/8 cup dried; 1/4 to 1/2 cup juice

- Meat/poultry/fish, eggs, and beans: two servings per day
  One serving = 2 tablespoons ground or 2 one-inch cubes meat, poultry, or fish; one egg; 1/4 cup tofu or cooked beans

Depending upon everyone's schedule, make an effort to include your toddler at the family table for at least one meal per day and let her see the family pause for a blessing. While not exactly participating at the same level as everyone around the table, your one-year-old will be watching and listening and will become accustomed to being included in these gatherings.

When should I start weaning my toddler from a bottle?

As the year progresses, you will see improving skill in your toddler's use of the cup and spoon, which will enable you to turn more of the feeding assignment over to her. With increasing cup proficiency, you can begin phasing out bottles. This process may meet with some resistance but should be started by the first birthday and accomplished by the fifteen-month mark. Plan on substituting a cup for her bottle one meal at a time (or all three at once, if you're adventurous), and then do likewise for her snacks.

Usually a bottle before bedtime is the last to go, since it has a way of becoming part of the nighttime routine. Remember: No milk or juice should ever be given to your baby while she is lying down and falling asleep because this practice (which is all too easy to start as a last resort during a restless night) can lead to dental cavities and ear infections. A little snack just before bed and before brushing teeth is fine, but food should not be part of any middle-of-the-night activity at this point.

Once you've decided to bid the last bottle feeding farewell, your best bet is to pack all the bottles away when your toddler is asleep. If she begins to ask (or cry) for her "baba," be matter-of-fact and upbeat: "Your bottles are gone! And you're so big, you don't need them anymore!"

If your baby is still nursing at this point and has never used a bottle, she can graduate directly from breast to cup and avoid bottles altogether. You should still introduce your baby to drinking from a cup even if most of her fluids are coming directly from Mom. If you wait too long, you may face resistance when it's time to stop nursing.

What can I expect when my toddler spends time with other children?

Very often two or more sets of parents who have toddlers of similar ages will have the bright idea of getting their offspring together for a little fun and group playtime. After all, isn't this a good time to learn how to get along and make new friends?

Believe it or not, the answer is "probably not," *especially* if the children are closer to one than to two years old.

With rare exception, a one-year-old is incapable of playing cooperatively with children her own age. Her universe is centered around herself, and she cannot comprehend such niceties as understanding the viewpoint or feelings of someone else. Parents and other adult caregivers are important to her, of course, but another small child will generate little more interest than another toy—except when each is interested in the same item.

If there's one concept that is foreign to the toddler's outlook, it is sharing. She cannot grasp the idea that one of her toys can be "borrowed" or used by someone else and still remain hers, or vice versa. She lives in the here and now, and "waiting a turn" is a meaningless phrase. Therefore, if you turn more than one toddler loose in the same room, keep a close watch and plan to serve as referee. Having plenty of toys available will help, of course, but you will need to be ready to intervene at the first sign of combat. This is important not only as a means of keeping the flow of tears to a minimum but also to prevent physical consequences. All too often if a desired item can't be pulled easily out of the grip of another child, pushing and hitting will follow.

Should this occur, separate the opponents with a clear rebuke ("No hitting!"), tend to any wounds, and then administer consequences. In this case, immediate withdrawal of a privilege (such as access to the toy she wanted) or a time of isolation from the others and the toys is an appropriate response.

If the skirmish includes biting, you will need to take decisive action to reduce the risk of a repeat performance, because human bite wounds carry a significant risk of infection. The biter should be removed from the scene and given a firm, eyeball-to-eyeball order: "Do not bite Amanda or anyone else! Biting hurts very much." A long lecture about manners or infections isn't necessary, but you may want to maintain a steady (but not painful) grip on the upper body to prevent any wiggling or movement for a minute or so. A toddler normally becomes quite unhappy after a very short period of this restraint, and continuing it for fifteen to thirty seconds after she begins to complain will reinforce your point. (Say it again before you let go.) Do not shake or slap her, and never bite the biter in an effort to show "how bad it feels."

Along with maintaining zero tolerance for your child's biting anyone, consider some preventive measures as well. If you hear a conflict brewing between two toddlers, don't wait for them to negotiate through their disagreement because they can't (and won't) at this age. Distract, separate, take whatever is in dispute out of the picture, or simply call it a day if it looks as if everyone is tired and cranky.

How can I help my older child get along with my toddler?

Depending upon the spacing of your children, conflict between a toddler and other siblings is virtually inevitable. If your children are spaced less than two years apart, the older at first will be wary of the attention being showered on the younger and may even regress to babylike behavior in an effort to regain center stage.

Once she is assured of her place in your affection, however, she probably will pay little attention to the baby—until he becomes mobile. Once this happens, the insatiable curiosity of the new explorer will inevitably lead to an invasion of big sister's possessions. If your older child isn't yet two and a half, don't expect her to embrace any high-minded ideals about sharing. Try to keep your older child's prized possessions out of harm's way, and in return, make it clear that any hitting or other physical action taken against the younger sibling will have unpleasant consequences.

Even with very basic ground rules, however, some combat is inevitable. Furthermore, when it erupts, you may not always be able to figure out who did what to whom or who was at fault. This problem often gives parents considerable grief, and you will need plenty of wisdom, prayer, and patience to deal with it. In general, your response will have to depend on the age of the children involved. With very young children, separation from one another and whatever they were fighting over should be your most common tactic. Remember that this age-group is not terribly responsive to logic and reason. Later on, more sophisticated ground rules, "rules of evidence" when stories contradict, and consequences that fit the crime will need to be carried out.

If there is a difference of a few years or more between children, the likelihood of conflict with a toddler will be reduced. Not only will the older child have her own circle of friends and interests, but depending on her age, she may serve, at least at times, as a caregiver. She should not, however, be given disciplinary authority or responsibilities that belong to you alone.

What about training and disciplining a child at this age?

Between a baby's eighth and fifteenth months, some limit setting must begin as she becomes more mobile. However, an intense desire to explore her surroundings is normal, and her fierce determination to do so should not be interpreted as defiance. The primary methods to utilize at this age are baby-proofing and distraction, which are preferable to a steady diet of No's! from parents and older children.

During these months (and up to about age three), your expectations for your child's behavior should focus on her safety as well as on preventing her from harming people or things around her. Specific goals for her should include coming when called, responding to simple directions (such as not touching things that are off-limits), and not hitting or biting anyone. However, you cannot expect a child this age to sit still for long periods of time or to be affectionate with someone on cue. It is also futile to force a child this age (or any other) to consume food you have placed before her.

As she continues to grow and mature, you will have to deal with numerous episodes of *childish irresponsibility*—knocking over the milk or leaving toys all over the living room, for example—that need correction but usually do not represent a direct challenge to your authority. On some occasions, however, the issue will be *willful defiance.* This can begin surprisingly early—between fifteen and eighteen months of age.

Willful defiance takes place when your child (1) knows and clearly understands what you want (or don't want) to happen, (2) is capable of doing what you want, and (3) refuses to do so. Whether passive or "in your face," the defiant child is asking several questions: Do Mom and Dad really mean business? What's going to happen if I don't do what they want? Who's really in charge here?

When confronted with such a situation, act clearly and decisively. Not only must your child not have her way, but her attitude about what she has done must be turned around as well. You don't need to be harsh or hostile, but you must not back down. *If you do not establish your right to lead early in the game (by the age of two or three at the latest), your ability to influence or control your child later on will be seriously compromised.*

What specific disciplinary measures are appropriate for toddlers and young children?

In most situations, words are all the response you will need. For toddlers and small children, a disapproving look and a tone of voice that says you mean business will often promptly change behavior. For the toddler, simple statements such as "Don't touch the stove," especially when accompanied by physically lifting him away from it, are appropriate.

Withholding a privilege can be effective during toddlerhood and beyond. If your toddler bangs a toy against the coffee table despite your clear direction to stop, put the toy away for a while.

Time-out can be useful with toddlers, preschoolers, and early grade-school children, especially when emotions need to cool down. This involves isolating the child in a playpen, in his room, or simply on a chair for a specified period of time. Usually one minute of time-out per year of age is appropriate, although if he hasn't calmed down, more time may be necessary. This approach is usually effective, assuming that the child is willing to cooperate. If he refuses to stay on the chair or starts trashing his room during a time-out, more direct physical intervention may be necessary.

Disciplinary spanking is a tool that can be useful in specific circumstances. Some voices in our culture condemn spanking, and their concerns are valid for abusive forms of corporal punishment (such as slapping or beating), in cases where spanking is an expression of anger and frustration, or when it causes injury. But when utilized appropriately, spanking can and should be neither abusive nor damaging to a child's well-being.

A disciplinary spanking should be administered only in response to an episode of willful defiance characterized by a clear, appropriate parental directive that the child understands and is capable of following; a direct challenge from the child, especially with a disrespectful or hostile tone; or persistent and blatant refusal to cooperate. Any physical action you take should not be an outpouring of anger, but rather a tactic to turn your child's behavior around and bring the rebellion to a swift conclusion. One to three quick swats should provide a brief, superficial sting to the buttocks or the back of the upper thighs. It should be just hard enough to get his attention, bring on some tears, and break through the defiance, but it should not cause bruising or other damage to the skin. (You should try your method of choice on your own skin first.) The use of hardware such as heavy belts or canes, as well as other forms of violence such as face slapping or punching, have no place in the rearing of a child.

A disciplinary spanking should be carried out in private, between parent and child. It must be followed by reconciliation, comforting, and simple teaching about how to avoid such an episode in the future. *You should not need to take this course of action more than a few times during your child's life.* Once you have established clearly that you are in charge, many (if not most) episodes of defiance can be settled using other measures, such as verbal reprimands, time-outs, or restriction of privileges.

Disciplinary spanking should not be carried out:

- if you feel angry, highly stressed, or emotionally unstable;

- if you were abused as a child, unless you have worked through your past hurts (and the issue of corporal punishment of your own children) with a professional counselor;

- if you are not clear about the difference between childish irresponsibility and willful defiance;

- if parents are not in agreement about its appropriate use.

What do I need to know to keep my child safe at this age?

Because of your child's maturing motor and problem-solving skills, your vigilance for his ongoing safety must not only continue but become more sophisticated. His developing fine-motor coordination will include new abilities that can lead to new hazards: turning doorknobs, manipulating latches, flipping switches, and pushing buttons. If you turn your back for a moment, he may be locked in the bathroom or out the door and down the street, peering over the edge of Grandma's swimming pool. His interest in climbing to precarious new heights may increase, along with his ability to find new and clever ways to get to them.

His tendency to gum everything as a means of gathering information will wane, but he may not hesitate to place small objects in his mouth. Remember to stay vigilant for any such items that might cause choking if accidentally inhaled. He may very well take a swig or a bite of *anything* that looks interesting. Medicines, plants, cleaning products, dog food—you name it—nothing is off-limits for an oral sampling. You cannot assume that a bad taste will keep him from guzzling the furniture polish or anything else. This year and the next are the most risky for your child accidentally ingesting a dangerous substance. Some basic precautions can help you and your toddler avoid the trauma of a poisoning incident:

- Keep household products (cleaners, antifreeze, drain openers, pesticides, kerosene, and many others) and medicines in latched or locked cabinets or drawers, preferably at levels beyond a child's reach.

- Always label hazardous products clearly.

- Avoid referring to a child's medicine as "candy" or "a treat" when you're trying to get him to take it. If it tastes good, he might decide to try some on his own.

- Be sure to replace childproof caps on medications immediately after use.

- Be especially careful when you are using one or more hazardous products during a lengthy household project. When tired or distracted, you might lose track of what you have left lying within reach of curious hands.

How do I establish—and maintain—a sleeping routine?

By his first birthday, your child will likely have been sleeping through the night for some time. If not, remember that by now his nocturnal awakenings aren't the result of any nutritional needs. Instead, he has learned that having company or a snack feels good during the night. Why go back to sleep after awakening momentarily in the wee hours when there are other pleasantries to enjoy?

If you really don't mind working the nursery night shift, you may choose to put off dealing with the inevitable protest that will break forth when you cancel room service. But if he is otherwise well, you can usually establish uninterrupted sleep for everyone within one or two days, typically over a weekend, once you decide to take the plunge. (See chapter 3, pages 76–78, for details).

Even a seasoned all-night sleeper, however, may depart from his pattern during an illness, while on a trip, after a move, or perhaps because of a bad dream. Under these circumstances, you'll need to provide care and comfort (though not snacks, unless you have been specifically directed by the doctor to push fluids when he is sick) until things settle down, then nudge him back toward his old habits.

At some point, you're likely to run into bedtime resistance, manifested either by winsome appeals (requests for another kiss, one last drink, and in subsequent months, answers to riddles of the universe) or by outright rebellion against getting or staying in bed. Some of this may arise from separation anxiety, from negativism, or simply from the fact that other people are up doing interesting things, and lying in a crib or bed seems awfully boring by comparison. You may be tempted to take the path of least resistance and let him decide when he's ready to sleep—in other words, when he eventually collapses from sheer exhaustion. This is a bad idea for a number of reasons:

- You need to spend time with older children (if you have any) without an increasingly tired and irritable toddler wandering around.

- You need to spend time with your mate or by yourself without any children wandering around.

- Your toddler needs the sleep—a good ten or eleven hours at night—which probably won't happen if he's staying up until your bedtime.

If not already in place, establishing both a fixed bedtime and a fixed bedtime routine will be an important task this year. Even if his vocabulary is limited, you can talk him through the steps you choose: bath, jammies, story, song, prayer, for example, carried out in a manner that winds him down. A raucous wrestling match or chasing the dog right before bedtime probably won't help set the stage for turning in. Keep in mind that whatever bedtime routine you establish (including one that takes one or two hours to complete) may become entrenched and expected every night for years to come.

At the first birthday, most children are still logging three to four hours of daytime sleep, usually in two naps. The amount of daytime sleep will decline to two or three hours over the next year, and as a result, the morning nap will eventually phase out. When your toddler shifts to a one-nap-per-day routine, don't start too late in the afternoon or you may increase his bedtime resistance. (Who wants to go to bed after just getting up?) And though he may seem intent on playing through the entire afternoon, don't be conned into eliminating nap time altogether, even if he resists it. Without daytime sleep, afternoons will probably be more notable for combat than for companionship.

What can I expect at my child's health checkups this year?

Your toddler should have a routine exam at age one, at fifteen and eighteen months, and at age two. As before, along with the normal gentle poking and prodding, his measurements will be taken and charted, and his developmental milestones (walking, etc.) should be reviewed.

Don't expect a great deal of cooperation from your toddler during these exams. Typically the same physician who was greeted with coos a few months ago will now elicit howls of terror. Most of the exam will need to be done with your child sitting on your lap, and at times (such as when his ears are being checked) you will need to hold him still, pinning arms and head to your chest in an affectionate hammerlock. Occasionally, a more prolonged look into the ears will be needed, especially when wax needs to be cleared, and you may be asked to help keep your screaming and thrashing patient quite still on the exam table while this is going on. You will be impressed at how strong your child is, how upset he sounds, and how guilty you feel. Remember, however, that he is experiencing far more fright than pain.

Everyone will have an easier time at the doctor's office if you can maintain a cheerful and confident demeanor throughout the visit. If your toddler senses that you are apprehensive or ambivalent about what is going on, his fright level may increase tenfold. When he cries or resists, don't plead with him to stop. Keep your voice mellow and reassuring, and your grip tight.

Between twelve and fifteen months of age, your child should receive a number of immunizations, including some that are new to him as well as booster doses and any catch-up shots that he needs. These are likely to include vaccines against measles, mumps, rubella, varicella (chickenpox), and hepatitis A; boosters to protect against tetanus, diphtheria, pertussis (whooping cough), pneumococci, and *Haemophilus influenzae* type B; and any remaining doses of the hepatitis B or polio series if either wasn't completed during the first year. In addition, a dose of influenza vaccine is recommended every year in the fall for all children six months or older.

If you haven't done so already, be sure to make an appointment for your toddler to see a dentist who cares for children.

Is it time to start potty training?

Probably not. Some children may show signs that they are ready to learn this skill before the second birthday, and you may begin the process of training them if you desire. But most toddlers are still in the throes of discovering their place in the world and dealing with their emotions during this eventful year, and adding any pressure to get rid of diapers and use the toilet may create even more turmoil. Take your time.

CHAPTER 6

TWO-YEAR-OLDS

ALTHOUGH YOU HAVE probably heard the phrase "terrible twos" more often than you care to remember, the birthday cake with two candles on it shouldn't create a feeling of impending doom. True, your two-year-old may be working through the negativism of his "first adolescence" in all its defiant glory. Yes, you will have days when he runs headlong away from you when you call him, then later clings to you like Velcro when you want to leave him with a trusted caregiver for an hour. And yes, your two-year-old is bigger, stronger, and faster than he was six months ago, and he is probably turbocharged with energy much of the day. And to be sure, if you have a new baby who is starting to be more mobile and is becoming a bigger blip on your two-year-old's radar screen, you can count on some fireworks erupting between them.

But while you have your work cut out for you in many respects, you will also have the privilege of watching some incredible developments in language, thinking, and creativity unfold during this twelve-month period. The transition from infant to child will be completed by the third birthday, and with this transition will come the joy of having more complex interactions and sustained companionship with him.

What physical developments will I see at this age?

A weight gain of about four pounds (1.8 kg) and the addition of two-and-a-half to three-and-a-half inches (about 6½ to 9 cm) in height can be expected this year. A popular notion holds that your child will have reached half of his adult height by the age of two. While you may get a general idea of his ultimate altitude by doubling his height at twenty-four months, don't start buying his high school wardrobe quite yet. Differences in nutritional and hormonal patterns may hand you a surprise during the teen years, especially if the onset of puberty is either quite early or delayed.

The gradual change in the overall shape of your child's body that began last year will become more obvious. The size of his arms, legs, and upper body will increase much more than his head as he loses the top-heavy proportions of an infant. His posture will become more erect and stable, his abdomen less prominent, and his back straighter. Baby fat will continue to disappear, replaced by more grown-up contours.

His body movements, which are already perpetual, will also become much more sophisticated. By the third birthday he will be able to run, jump, climb up or down stairs while holding your hand or the rail, stand on one foot (if you demonstrate), and do any number of things with his hands while walking. During the course of this year he will discover the pleasure of maneuvering up and down a small slide, kicking a ball, and pedaling a small tricycle.

As his capacity for vigorous activity continues to increase, you will want to find a pleasant and safe outdoor environment where he can discharge some of his boundless energy every day.

But whether in your own yard, a greenbelt, or a local park, you must continuously keep track of his activities and explorations and not merely turn him loose without supervision. Indeed, he will be delighted if you join him in whatever tumbling, chasing, or piggyback pursuits he enjoys.

As during his first months of crawling and toddling, his judgment at this age will be no match for his physical capabilities. This is especially true around bodies of water such as spas and swimming pools, which must be securely gated or otherwise inaccessible. *Never* underestimate the ability of your two-year-old to climb onto, into, or under whatever hazardous place he can find.

Along with his full-body activities, his coordination of hand, wrist, and finger movements will also improve. Given a pencil or crayon, he will be happy to scribble at age two and will add circular motions to his artistic repertoire by age three, even attempting to represent some object on the page. Be sure to ask him what it is and be prepared for some wonderful and unique explanations. Write down what he says on the back of his masterpiece, along with the date. After a decade or so passes, these small treasures will spark sweet memories.

Your child will also learn to turn the pages of a book one at a time, turn doorknobs and handles, and unscrew lids, by the end of this year. He will also begin to enjoy stacking and building with blocks.

How will my child's language progress at two years of age?

During the next twelve months, you can expect an enormous increase in the number of words your child can speak and understand. You should be aware, however, that normal children will vary significantly in the use of language at this age. Some will seem to pick up new vocabulary day by day, while others may say little for weeks, then surprise you with a complete and quite expressive sentence. As a general estimate, your child will arrive at her second birthday with the ability to use about fifty words, some of which will be connected in two-word sentences ("Doggy jump!"). She will, however, *understand* about three hundred words. By the third birthday, roughly one thousand words will be in her memory bank, and sentences of four to six words (including pronouns such as *I* or *you*) will be forthcoming.

In addition to learning the meanings of hundreds of new words, your child will also begin to pick up other important information about how words are assembled and in what tone of voice they are used. Are your family's conversations calm and laced with respectful and soothing phrases, or do they sound like a cross between a barracks and a back alley? If you don't believe your child is tuned in to your language, wait until she repeats some choice comment she overheard last week—just when the pastor stops by for a visit.

How do I take care of my child's teeth?

Between eighteen and thirty months of age, all twenty of the primary ("baby") teeth will have arrived. Although they will all be replaced, secondary (permanent) teeth won't appear for a few more years, so primary teeth deserve attention and care. (If a tooth becomes injured, see a dentist immediately. Sometimes it is possible to save damaged teeth.) Their biggest enemy will be decay, or caries, which affects many children by the age of three. If damage from caries is severe enough to cause the loss of any primary teeth, proper alignment of the permanent teeth may be affected later on.

There are four ways to reduce the likelihood of decay.

- Check with your child's health-care provider about the use of fluoride.

- Have your child checked regularly by a dentist who sees children (pedodontist).

- Your toddler won't be adept at handling a toothbrush, so you will need to do the honors with a soft brush at least once a day, usually at bedtime.

- Finally, don't let your toddler become hooked on foods that will provide a playground for destructive bacteria.

How will my child's eating routine change at two years of age?

Many of the recommendations about foods and snacks presented in the previous chapter apply to your two-year-old as well, and reviewing them now would be a good idea. The variations on the basic themes are as follows:

Offer a few more calories. As was the case a year ago, your two-year-old does not need a huge number of calories to grow and fuel her full-throttle engine. Roughly 1,200 to 1,400 calories per day—which won't seem like much—will do, spread out over three meals and one or two snacks. Don't bother trying to count or regulate these calories, by the way, unless your child has an unusual medical problem that requires nutritional oversight by a registered dietitian. Unless a risky metabolic problem (such as an inherited tendency to develop very high cholesterol levels and heart disease at an early age) has been diagnosed, a restricted-fat diet is neither necessary nor appropriate in this age-group because of the importance of dietary fat for the developing brain.

What matters now (and for years to come) is that you provide a variety of high-quality foods for everyone in your family, including your two-year-old.

One quantity you will want to track is milk intake, which at this age should be at least sixteen ounces and not more than thirty-two ounces per day, in order to supply enough calcium for growing bones without interfering with her appetite for other types of food. Between one and three years of age, your toddler needs about 500 mg of calcium per day; eight ounces (one cup) of milk supplies about 300 mg. (If your child won't drink or doesn't tolerate milk, you will need to offer and encourage other high-calcium foods such as cheese, yogurt, leafy green vegetables, and perhaps calcium-containing orange juice.)

At this age, you can offer any form of milk from whole to skim, and your best bet is to pick one concentration for the entire family to use. (Usually 1 or 2 percent offers the most agreeable compromise between calories and taste.) Remember that fat content doesn't affect the amount of calcium in milk.

Avoid bringing up a junkaholic or a food hermit. Over the next year and thereafter, your child will be exposed to a whole new world of commercial food products with more sugar, salt, and fat than she should eat on a regular basis. In light of this reality, you will need to avoid two extremes.

First, don't let her sway your food-preparation choices by persistent requests or demands for Chocolate Frosted Gonzo Flakes or Cheddar-Ecstasy Dip Chips. Stick with the basics when you buy and serve foods, and then stand your ground. On the other hand, don't become a dietary diehard, a purist who won't allow your child to go anywhere that doesn't serve food that is hand-grown, organically fertilized, homemade, unrefined, and 100 percent free of sugar. Your child can't live in a nutritional glass bubble, and it won't kill her if she has a couple of french fries or some birthday cake at a friend's party as long as food allergies are not an issue.

Utensils will be under better control, but not all foods are safe. During this year your child will master the use of both spoon and fork, relieving you completely of the duty of transferring food from her plate to her mouth. She will become adept at using a cup with one hand. However, she still isn't free from the risk of choking on the same foods that were hazardous last year: seeds, nuts, grapes, popcorn, celery, and little hard candies. Hot dogs and carrots should also be off-limits unless cut into very small pieces.

How can I avoid a power struggle at mealtime?

If there is one arena in which a two-year-old has nearly as much autonomy as she would like, it is in eating. If she won't swallow it, you can't make her, and you shouldn't try. There are more important battles to win.

For the next several months, you may wonder if your child is getting enough to eat, because often she may refuse to consume foods you place in front of her. But a child at this age may be an eager eater at only one meal a day. If she doesn't take much at lunch, she'll probably make up for it at dinner or the following day. Don't ruin a meal by nagging, bribing, or punishing a toddler who isn't interested in food.

Don't be extorted into preparing a separate toddler meal containing food that is different from everyone else's. Your job is to serve your two-year-old modest servings of wholesome foods that cover the gamut of the major food groups. Your child's job is to decide how much she'll actually eat. If she begins to push you for something else, hold the line. She won't starve.

If you are truly worried about your child's nutritional well-being, write down what she eats for a few days and then take this list to her physician. A check of height and weight and a brief exam will usually clear the air. A child who is in trouble medically usually shows other signs of illness: fever, diarrhea, lethargy, or poor weight gain, for example. A child who doesn't eat much but is otherwise very active is most likely getting enough food.

What are some special safety concerns for my two-year-old?

Your two-year-old is as intensely curious about the world around her as she was last year, but her methods of gathering and processing information are now more sophisticated. At this point she should be moving well beyond random touching, grabbing, banging, and gumming everything in sight. Instead, her efforts will become more focused and purposeful as she spends more time manipulating objects with her mind as well as her hands.

Traffic hazards. Because she can run more swiftly and dart into the nearest street, she must be monitored at all times when she is in an area where there are no barriers separating her from traffic. Also, be watchful of your child in parking lots.

Harmful substances. Medications must remain completely inaccessible, especially if they happen to be liquid and pleasantly flavored. Not only is she more skillful with the use of her hands, but her pretending games or imitation—new and important behaviors at this age—may include scenarios of playing doctor or taking medicines to get well. The use of ipecac to induce vomiting after an accidental ingestion is no longer recommended. Instead, if you suspect that your toddler has swallowed a toxic substance, do the following:

- Call the toll-free number for the US Poison Control Center at **1-800-222-1222** for advice if she doesn't appear ill.

- Call **911** immediately if she is unconscious, breathing erratically, or having convulsions. If she has stopped breathing, you must begin CPR while someone calls 911.

Car-seat struggles. She may become more vocal in protesting the use of her car seat, or she may actually figure out how to get out of it at some choice moment. Don't give an inch on your insistence that the seat be used for every ride in the car, no matter how short.

Dangerous "grown-up toys." Never underestimate her ingenuity in getting her hands on appliances, tools, or other hardware that she has seen you use. Imitation may come into play here as well.

The bathtub. She is still too young to be left in a tub unsupervised. The physical prowess that now makes shallow water seem less hazardous also enables her to turn on the faucet, leading to a possible scalding injury or an overflowing tub. (Lowering the temperature of your water heater below 120°F [49°C] will reduce the risk of scalding.) She might also decide to see what happens when she jumps up and down in the water—and in so doing, slip and fall.

Other water hazards. Nonstop watchfulness is an absolute necessity whenever your two-year-old is near a swimming pool or any other body of water. Curiosity is abundant and caution scarce at this age, and a child can make a beeline toward a body of water in just a few moments while you are distracted with something else. As stated earlier, if you have a pool at home, it is essential that a childproof fence—at least four feet high, not climbable, and equipped with a self-closing and self-latching gate—surrounds it. A spa or hot tub must be covered when not in use. If your child is playing in water, he must be observed by a responsible individual—ideally by someone who is in the water with him—at all times. Do not rely on inner tubes, water wings, or other flotation devices to keep your child safe.

Sibling skirmishes. Be on the lookout for impending aggression toward siblings, both older and younger. Whether or not your two-year-old is the one who initiates the conflict, her ability to inflict damage is ever increasing.

How will my child's play change at this age?

One of the fascinating developments of a two-year-old's emerging intellect is the capacity for imitation, role-playing, and make-believe. Watch her be a mommy to one of her dolls or pretend to drive her toy car around the carpet or collect some of her animals into a miniature zoo, and you can learn a lot about what she's thinking.

A normal and important component of this phase is imitating parents, especially the one of the same gender. Listen to her give an exhortation to her favorite stuffed animal, and you may hear words, phrases, and even vocal inflections that sound amazingly familiar. You may even see a little mirror of yourself in a young child's stride or in her hand gestures. This imitation is, in fact, normal and healthy—provided, of course, that what your child sees is worth copying. Character traits that are on display at home—whether respect, courtesy, stability, and love, or their opposites—are all being watched and assimilated, no matter who is modeling them.

Parents often wonder whether they should try to influence the type of role-playing their child carries out. In bygone generations some might have fussed and fumed, usually in vain, if Johnny played house and Susie pretended to be a train engineer. Today some cultural forces push parents and preschools—with equal fervor and futility—to keep children "gender neutral" in their play roles. In fact, at this age kids will gravitate toward the types of toys and play activities they find interesting, no matter what you do.

You should monitor more closely the *attitudes* that are being manifested in the pretending. Are you generally seeing and hearing pleasant themes and variations on your family's activities and interests? Or are you noticing some disturbing trends, focused more on violence and destruction? If you don't like what you're seeing, you may want to take stock of the material to which your two-year-old is exposed.

This is the time to become particularly attentive to the role of television in your child's life, not to mention your own. A year ago your walking baby didn't show much sustained interest in TV. But two-year-olds can become captivated by the stories and images they see on the flickering screen, and by age three, they can become TV addicts. Furthermore, a huge variation exists in the quality and appropriateness of network and cable programming geared toward children.

While you may find material that is nourishing to your child's mind and heart, far too much children's TV is deplorable—violent, occultic, manipulative, dumb, and dumber. In addition, many classic films for children are far too intense for two- or three-year-olds. In fact, the American Academy of Pediatrics (AAP) has flatly stated that the amount of time a child under two should spend watching a video screen is *zero* minutes per day. This recommendation has met with skepticism from many busy parents. Without being paranoid or overly legalistic, however, now is the time to get a firm grip on what you allow into your home and your child's mind.

How does a typical two-year-old interact with other children?

One obvious setting in which you will want to keep track of your two-year-old's playing and pretending is in the company of other children. Remember that as a one-year-old it would have been unusual for your child to engage in interactive play with another toddler her age. They might have played alongside one another, noting any potential threats to their possessions (which for each included everything in the room), but cooperative ventures would have been rare indeed.

As she passes her second birthday and moves toward her third, however, the possibility for more cooperative, interactive play with peers definitely increases. Ideally this will include situations in which she sets the pace ("Let's play with this now . . .") and others in which she follows another child's lead. Whether or not she can strike a healthy balance between leading and following other children will depend, in part, on the flavor of her relationships at home. If she is consistently loved and respected, she will be more likely to feel confident and friendly with other children and content to interact with them in a variety of ways. But if she has received the messages that she isn't worth much and that the world in which she lives is dangerous and unpredictable, she may shy away from dealing with other children or may be easily bullied. In the same way, seeing the adults at home overpowering others with loud voices and threatening actions may inspire her to adopt a similar aggressive approach to her peers or younger children.

If she believes that she rules the world (or at least everyone who crosses her path), her interactions with peers will probably be stormy, unless the others are willing to play servants while she continues her starring role as Queen of Everything. But when she has learned about meaningful limits and knows that she can't get her way through whining, yelling, hitting, grabbing, or other negative behaviors, she'll be less likely to try these out on other children.

But no matter how flawlessly she has been reared, the virtue of sharing with peers—or anyone else—will probably *not* become part of your child's repertoire until sometime around the third birthday. Sharing is still not an easy concept to grasp at this age for a number of reasons: The inborn, primitive self-centeredness of infancy and toddlerhood doesn't wane easily; patience is in short supply at age two; and it takes a while to grasp the idea that something given up now can be retrieved later.

How do I deal with my two-year-old's emotions?

Many parents approach this period of their child's life with a mixture of eager expectancy and dread. There's a real person emerging here, and it's exciting to see how he's going to develop. But in reflecting on the nonstop activity and the limit testing that went on during the previous year, you may be less than enthusiastic about the prospect of both perpetual motion and perpetual *e*-motion.

Like the adolescent, the two-year-old is undergoing major changes in his body and mind; he is still learning about the limits of his power and independence, and he tends to *feel* intensely about nearly everything. If he likes something, he can be ecstatic about it. If he loses or breaks it, the world might as well be coming to an end. If some task or toy frustrates him, he may fly into a rage. If he wants something and you won't let him have it, you may be shocked by the intensity of his reaction.

You might be reassured (or dismayed) to know that this is not only common but is, in fact, a warm-up for similar events—with a much bigger child—ten to twelve years from now. Even if you were consistent in contending with his negativism last year and have established a clear understanding that you care deeply about him but you are in charge, you still need to be prepared for some flare-ups. If he is still entrenched in a major power struggle with you as he passes his second birthday, you should make it a top priority to set up your boundaries in love—and concrete.

How should I deal with a full-blown tantrum?

When actually faced with one of these episodes, you will need to determine what works best for you and your child. This will depend to some extent on the cause. If it appears that the blowup has been brought on by factors such as fatigue, hunger, lack of sleep, or perhaps too much stimulation for one day—for example, an outburst occurs at the end of a long afternoon at an amusement park—you should try not only to deal with the spectacle in front of you but also to look for ways to cool off what is fueling it. (This may be easier said than done, especially in the heat of the moment.)

Depending upon your assessment, calm but firm measures such as getting him to a quiet place or putting him down for a nap may be helpful. If your child's emotional fuse always seems to get short under specific circumstances—perhaps at a certain time of day such as late afternoon or before a meal or at the end of a long car ride—you may want to adjust activities to reduce the likelihood of a repeat performance.

If the tantrum is born out of frustration with a toy or game whose proper use is beyond him, your best bet is to put the offending object away and try to distract your toddler with something else. But if the angry outburst is primarily an attempt to influence you to do something or to change your mind, you must be firm in your resolve never to allow any decision to be altered by a tantrum. If you give an inch, you can plan on many repeat performances.

Whatever is provoking and fueling a tantrum—whether physical factors beyond your child's control, the frustrations and conflicts of toddlerhood, or a deliberate attempt to manipulate the nearest adult—you still have to deal with it. Some have argued that a tantrum needs an audience and that ignoring it will therefore serve to remove fuel from the fire. If the outburst is at home and you can walk away, this approach may work. Make it clear that you will talk to him when he quiets down and not before. A variation on this theme suggests isolating the tantrum thrower in his room until he calms down.

But sometimes ignoring the tantrum won't be appropriate. If he is sounding off in the church foyer, turning away will prolong a disturbance that is disruptive to others. In this case, bodily removal to a quiet, private area followed by a more direct intervention is appropriate. If he is clearly trying to manipulate or goad you, a judicious swat or two on the behind followed by a calm explanation of how the problem can be avoided in the future will be more likely to bring the incident to a conclusion. On the other hand, if he is beside himself, flailing wildly and out of control, containing him in a bear hug until he calms down may be more appropriate. Whatever action you take, you must not allow the threat or eruption of a tantrum to torpedo your plans, whether in church, a restaurant, the mall, or anywhere else.

Another situation in which you cannot ignore a tantrum thrower is when he is causing damage. You might put him in his room to cool down, but what if he starts kicking the door or smashing the furniture? Or what if he delivers a swift kick to the dog or yanks his sister's hair? Once again, some form of direct intervention will be necessary. Trying to have a rational conversation in such situations is fruitless, negotiating is inappropriate, and asking or pleading for him to stop is disastrous. Protection of people and property and swift action to bring the episode to a close (including administration of consequences) take the highest priority. Discussions should begin only when the child is back under control.

If your two-year-old suddenly seems to be having tantrums more frequently with little or no provocation, consider having his health-care provider take a look at him to rule out a medical problem.

Another less dramatic but equally important form of emotional output is the verbal insult or disrespectful gesture. If you have a disagreement with your two-year-old and he lets fly with a choice comment such as "I hate you!" or "You're a doodoo-head," you should not punish him the *first* time. At this age he does not fully grasp the power of language, and it's your job to provide his first lessons. Sit him down, lock eyes with him, and explain clearly why such statements will be off-limits from now on. Let him know that it hurts you if he says he hates you, and that you will not allow him to call you names like "doodoo-head" or "dummy." The same should go for sticking out his tongue or aiming other disrespectful gestures in your direction.

Your two-year-old needs to begin learning the ABCs of what is, in fact, a sophisticated skill: how to express anger appropriately. Right now, virtually all of your input on this subject will be focused on what not to do—not to hit, bite, kick, throw or destroy things, launch a tantrum, or spew insults. When he is a little older, you can give him a basic but critically important message: *The way to express anger is in words that are not disrespectful to another person.*

How do I start potty training?

For many families, seeing a child graduate to a diaper-free lifestyle is as important a milestone as his unassisted first steps across the room. Like walking, toilet skills can't and won't happen until your child is good and ready. But unlike standing up and stepping out, the sequence of steps needed to send urine and stool from child to toilet isn't programmed into a toddler's brain. It needs to be taught by someone—usually one or both parents, although in large families older children sometimes teach the younger quite effectively.

When is it time to start this process? Some kids begin to master toilet skills between eighteen and twenty-four months of age, but it is uncommon for children to be diaper-free during the day by age two. The majority can be trained by thirty-six months, but for some children, daytime control may not be accomplished until the fourth birthday. Staying dry through the night may occur at the same time, but more often (for physiological reasons) dry mornings may not arrive until several months or even years later. Most children will learn to control bladder and bowel at the same time. However, for some, bowel control is easier to achieve, while for others, bowel control may lag several months behind.

Aside from his age, you should be on the lookout for indications that your child is ready to learn bladder and bowel control:

- He demonstrates some awareness that elimination (especially of stool) is going on. When a bowel movement is on its way, he may squat, grunt, grimace, or try to manipulate his diaper. Afterward he may be more insistent about getting cleaned up.

- The time between wet diapers is increasing. This indicates that a specific spinal-cord reflex, which automatically empties an infant's bladder whenever a certain amount of urine accumulates, is now being inhibited by signals from the brain. *No amount of training can speed up this neurological development.*

- He is able to understand and carry out two or three simple commands in sequence.

- He tries to imitate some of the things you do every day. You will want to take advantage of this normal behavior of two-year-olds during the toilet-training process.

- He is not embroiled in negativism. If his favorite word is still *no* and you're still neck deep in a daily struggle with him over who's in charge, this is not the best time to start a venture that requires as much cooperation as using the toilet.

In addition to your two-year-old being ready to learn, you must be ready to teach. While you undoubtedly would have been thrilled to see the last diaper disappear yesterday, be prepared to offer some patient, persistent, but relaxed attention to this project for as long as three to six months. This means that you should not be working under time pressure. All too often, potty training turns into a do-or-die crash course because one or both parents want their toddler in a preschool or day-care setting where diapers are off-limits. If you feel that somehow time is of the essence and find yourself impatient over your toddler's bathroom progress and exasperated when he has an accident, you may need to take a deep breath and reconsider your priorities.

If patience is not your virtue, you may want to start training later rather than sooner, when your child will have better comprehension, be more cooperative, and have fewer accidents. If you tend to be more laid-back, you may be able to try your luck with a younger trainee. You may find it easier to begin when the weather is warmer and there are fewer layers of clothing to worry about.

Once you feel that everyone is ready for the first day of potty school, you can begin a series of steps that will work most of the time. These may be stretched out over a period of several weeks or, for adventurous families with an agreeable toddler, compressed into a few days. Be prepared to adapt, revise, and adjust as you see fit. Above all, make sure you praise every step he takes in the right direction and don't show disappointment, dismay, or anger if he doesn't quite get what you're driving at. Punishment or harsh reprimands are counterproductive in teaching a child to use the toilet and should not be used.

Start talking about the process in an upbeat way. You will need to choose your vocabulary for these conversations with a little caution, since any particularly colorful words you use may be broadcast by your child in public, usually when least expected. Most families manage quite well with terms such as "pee," "peepee," or "tinkle" for urine and "poop" or "poopoo" for stool, with "going potty" designating the process of eliminating either. In most settings these terms won't raise any eyebrows but will communicate a child's needs with reasonable precision.

While you're changing a diaper, mention that soon he won't need diapers anymore and that he'll be using a potty just like Mom and Dad and his older siblings. You may want to read him a children's book about becoming potty trained (there are a number on the market) if you find it appropriate.

Let him become familiar with the sight of his own potty seat. If you buy one, let him help you pick it out. At the outset, a toddler-size seat that allows him to push against the floor while having a bowel movement is preferable to one that attaches to the big toilet but requires him to dangle his feet. You can make this item a familiar sight in the bathroom, although for safety reasons, your toddler should not be spending time there by himself if he has just turned two. As an alternative, the potty seat can be part of the furniture in his room for a while before he begins to use it.

Invite him to sit on the potty-chair. If he's willing, let him take this "test drive" without his pants and diaper on. If he's wary and reluctant, let him sit on it while still dressed. If you don't mind the temporary intrusion on your own bathroom time, you might have him sit on his throne while you sit on yours. For the sake of orienting him to some ground rules for modesty in the family, this part of the process would best be done with the parent of the same gender. Sharing potty time should be skipped if either parent (or the toddler) is uncomfortable with the idea.

A quick story might make the process more interesting to him. After he has done this several times and appears comfortable with it, have him sit on the toilet *without* his pants or diaper on. You don't need to prolong this exercise, but make it pleasant.

Let him see you empty stool from a soiled diaper into the receptacle of his potty-chair, while you explain that soon he will let his own "poop" drop in without the diaper. You may want to demonstrate how you flush his product down the toilet— but then again you may not, because your progress may become sidetracked by riddles of the universe ("Where does it go?"), deep concerns, or utter fascination with the loud noise and rushing rapids. Or (believe it or not) toddlers have been known to resist the idea that "part of them" suddenly just disappeared before their wondering eyes.

When you're ready to go for it, put him in loose pants that are easy to remove (or if you're feeling adventurous and can confine him to floors that are easy to wash, let him go bare). Watch for his telltale signs that a stool is coming 'round the bend, being especially vigilant thirty to sixty minutes after his biggest meal of the day. This takes advantage of the gastrocolic reflex, through which the stomach notifies the colon to get things moving because more digested food is on the way.

If you're not getting any obvious signals, place him on his potty every hour or two and encourage him to do his business. Take your time, look relaxed, chitchat, or even read part of a story if you'd like. If he succeeds, give him lots of praise. If he doesn't, don't worry about it—and don't become aggravated if he goes right after you get him off his potty. If he seems completely clueless about the whole project or you find yourself getting increasingly frustrated, go back to diapers for a while and try again later.

Usually urine will be released at the same time as stool, so both boys and girls typically learn to pass urine while sitting down. Sometime later, after control is well established, a boy can be shown (usually by Dad or an older brother) how to void while standing up.

Even after he has succeeded several times, you can continue to give him potty prompts during the day: when he gets up, after meals, before naps, on your way out the door, before bedtime—basically every couple of hours throughout the day. As he becomes more adept at this process and you are changing fewer moist or dirty diapers, you can graduate to training pants during the day and eventually during naps as well. If you so desire and both of you are ready, he can move to a kid-size training seat on the big toilet. When using this equipment, it will be easier for him to push during a bowel movement if you place a small stool under his feet.

Remember to instill some hygienic routines as part of your training program. Little girls should be taught to wipe from front to back for both urine and stool, in order to reduce the risk of bladder infections. Washing hands with soap after using the potty should become a habit. When your child uses public facilities, show him what he can and can't touch, and how to use the faucet/soap/paper towels/hand dryers after he has done his business.

Eventually he will use the potty at bedtime and wake up dry the next day, then triumphantly empty his bladder into the potty or big toilet. Give him lots of praise when this happens, but don't be discouraged if history doesn't repeat itself with total consistency.

The time it will take before you can count on dry diapers and then dry sheets every morning will vary enormously among children. For some, a combination of very deep sleep, weak inhibition of the bladder reflex, and other physiological factors will delay nighttime bladder control for years. Getting him up at night to stagger into the bathroom and use the potty in a dead sleep will not hasten the process. *Do not reprimand, humiliate, or punish a child who has trouble in this area because it is completely out of his control.* Not only will such measures fail to bring about the desired results, but they burden a child with needless shame, frustration, and ultimately resentment.

What kinds of sleeping problems can occur at this age?

Two-year-olds generally need nine to thirteen hours of sleep, most of which (eleven hours or thereabouts) occur during the night, with about a two-hour nap at midday. Some will still do best with two shorter naps, while others will regularly fight nap time with a vengeance. How long you continue a daytime sleep routine will depend upon its impact on your child. If he resists but eventually falls asleep for an hour or two, most likely a nap is worth maintaining. Similarly, if he turns into a three-foot-tall tyrant by the end of the day whenever he skips his nap, you should overrule his objections to a siesta. The time to phase out naps—whether this year or later—will arrive when he can regularly make it through the entire day without having a prolonged attitude meltdown.

Your more important assignment will be to maintain a bedtime routine in the face of increasing resistance, which in some children can become impressive. Some of the turbulence you may encounter at bedtime or during the night can arise from the following issues:

It's not his idea. Bedtime can be one of the great battlegrounds in a contest of wills between you and your child. You will certainly want to make sure that bedtime is a calm, relaxing, reassuring time of day and that other concerns are dealt with. But ultimately someone will have to decide when it's bedtime, and it shouldn't be your two-year-old.

Separation anxiety. Often this can be resolved by making sure that the bedtime routine isn't rushed; by providing security/comfort objects (a favorite toy or blanket); by playing quiet, soothing music in his room; or by leaving the door to his room open—provided that other sounds in the home won't keep him awake. If he hears the family having noisy fun without him, he will have little interest in lying down and closing his eyes.

Other fears. Your child may now become worried about scary sounds he hears, funny shapes in the closet, or darkness itself. A night-light in his room or light from the next room coming through an open doorway can be a calming fixture. Unexpected loud noises, such as a catfight outside his window, a siren passing nearby, or a booming thunderstorm, may frighten a small child and require some hands-on comforting.

Your two-year-old may also be unsettled about what went on during the day. Noisy arguments between parents are alarming, even when he can't understand their content. A move to new living quarters, a new baby in the house, the first trip to a preschool or day-care facility, or changes in family routines related to one or both parents' job schedules may also rock his sense of security. Ongoing overtures for attention at bedtime may signal a need for more (or more reassuring) attention during the daylight hours.

Night terrors. These unpleasant events, which affect up to 2 to 4 percent of children (more commonly boys), scare the daylights out of everyone who sees them. During the middle of the night a confused, wild-eyed child will suddenly begin screaming, kicking, thrashing, sweating, moaning, and jabbering incoherently. His heart will be pounding and his breathing will be rapid—and so will yours. He may climb out of bed, stumble around and injure himself, and if he is older, try to run out of the house. What is especially unsettling during a night terror is that your child won't respond to you or even seem to know you. When you attempt to calm him, he may thrash more violently and try to push you away.

Despite all of the wild activity, children do not actually awaken during a night terror. They are instead having a disordered arousal from deep sleep. The first episode occurs between the ages of two and four years, and other family members may have done the same thing during their toddler years.

Your job during a night terror is to sit tight through the interminable ten to thirty minutes, provide soothing reassurance that you're there and that he's okay, hold him if he'll let you, and most of all prevent him from hurting himself. You may also need to calm down any older children who have been awakened by the commotion and are witnessing this wild event. *Don't leave him alone* because there is a very real risk of injury, and *don't try to wake him up*. He is actually in a state of sleep that does not readily progress to wakefulness, and shaking or speaking forcefully to him ("Wake up! Wake up!") will only compound his (and your) agitation.

Furthermore, if you succeed in bringing him to full consciousness, he will be unhappy and irritable and may have difficulty going back to sleep. Instead, if you sit tight and stay cool, you will be surprised at how quickly the night terror ends once it has run its course. Your child will suddenly fall back to sleep, and in the morning he will have no memory of the previous night's uproar. You, on the other hand, may stare at the ceiling for a while as your adrenaline surge calms down.

Your child may have only one night terror, or you may have to endure many episodes before he outgrows them. Identifying a cause may be difficult, although it is possible that a sudden pain, such as a cramp in the abdomen, during the wrong phase of sleep may set off a night terror. In rare cases, night terrors may be frequent enough to require preventive medication prescribed by a physician.

Nightmares. These are different from night terrors in all respects. They are scary dreams, occurring during active sleep late in the night or very early in the morning. In contrast to the bug-eyed thrashing of the night terror, a child who cries out after a nightmare will be wide-awake, aware, and responsive to your presence and comfort. Instead of the sudden return to sleep that follows a night terror, a nightmare may leave a child unwilling or unable to fall back to sleep.

Whether or not he can tell you about the dream will depend upon his age and vocabulary. Even if he can't fill you in on the details, it's safe to assume that whatever he experienced was frightening and that his need for comfort is genuine. In particular he will need your reassurance that the dream was not real, a difficult concept to grasp at this age. A few moments of prayer can also help impart the idea that Jesus is truly in charge and looking after your child whether he's asleep or awake. Be sure, however, that you are not contributing to the problem by reciting "Now I Lay Me Down to Sleep." This poem's infamous lines "If I should die before I wake, I pray the Lord my soul to take" are not only alarming and inappropriate for children (and adults) but have no basis in Scripture or anywhere else.

How you deal with nightmares will depend on your perception of what is going on. A child who suddenly awakens at 4 a.m. crying and frightened will need conversation and cuddling. When he was younger, you may have worked diligently to end routine nighttime awakenings by holding back on "room service" during the wee hours. But after a real nightmare, that approach should be set aside.

Occasionally you may find it expedient to let him fall asleep in your bed if he won't calm down any other way. However, if he repeatedly wanders into the family room a half hour after bedtime and calmly announces that he "had a bad dream" or crawls into your bed night after night using "nightmare" as the password, he may be trying to change the bedtime ground rules, and a more businesslike approach will be needed.

Unlike night terrors, nightmares are influenced far more by daytime input. The old adage about turning off the scary movie because "it might give you nightmares" is certainly appropriate for small children, who cannot readily distinguish reality from fantasy. Because television, videos, DVDs, and video games can bring hair-raising images before your toddler's undiscerning eyes, you will need to exercise nonstop vigilance in this area. Even films such as *Pinocchio* or *Snow White*, widely considered to be childhood classics, contain sequences that could definitely scare a toddler.

How can I help my child make the transition from a crib to a bed?

This is one of the important transitions most two-year-olds must navigate. It will become necessary when the side rail of her crib reaches to less than three-quarters of her standing height (usually at about thirty-six inches), since the risk of scaling the rail and falling out increases after this point. The arrival of a younger sibling may also prompt the move.

The move to a bed can be a happy occasion, an indication that she is a "big girl" and no longer a baby. If she is unhappy about leaving the crib, affirming how grown-up she is may help change her opinion. You may help her gain more enthusiasm for moving to a bed if you let her help pick it out (assuming you are shopping for one) or at least choose a set of fun sheets and pillowcases to adorn her new sleeping quarters.

One potential drawback of a bed is that it allows your toddler to get up and come calling if she doesn't want to stay put. A more unsettling possibility is that your toddler may decide to wander around the house—or even go outside—when everyone is asleep. You may be able to limit these nighttime explorations (and certainly prevent accidental falls from bed) by installing a simple safety rail. However, a determined toddler can easily climb around the rail and get out of bed. For this reason, if size and circumstances permit, it may be wise to maintain the crib until she is closer to three years of age and possesses a little more wisdom and training. If you aren't already doing so, keep all doors and windows locked.

What should I expect at my two-year-old's medical visit?

Beginning at age two, routine medical checkups will take place every year. Whether or not your two-year-old will remain calm or become combative during the exam will depend on her temperament and her memory. One way to ease her apprehension is to bring a favorite stuffed animal or doll. Not only will this serve as a little piece of familiar landscape in a strange environment, but the doctor, physician assistant, or nurse practitioner may be willing to "examine" the toy along with your child. This will show her what's coming and provide some reassurance as well ("Minnie's heart sounds fine; now let's check yours"). If she wants to sit on your lap for the exam, let her. By next year, she'll probably be eager to climb up on the table by herself.

Remember to be completely straightforward about any shots or other procedures that your child may not like. If something is going to hurt, don't say it won't or your child won't believe you next time. She should know that it's okay to cry but that she needs to hold still. *Never say that the doctor is going to give her a shot if she doesn't behave.* It is vital that your child understand that medical procedures will never be done as a punishment but only because you and the doctor care about her.

Any advice on handling my own fatigue, relationships, and general outlook on life?

This year you will wonder at times why God didn't install roller skates on parents' feet, and you will perhaps wish you could get a transfusion of your child's energy. Indeed, ongoing fatigue is often an unwelcome companion during the eventful years of bringing up young children.

This energy deficit is particularly common among mothers of toddlers. For whether or not she stays at home with her young children, and whether or not she has a supportive husband who shares in the work of child rearing, much of the responsibility for caring and nurturing a young child will tend to fall on Mom. Furthermore, if there is a new baby in the family, Mom will be recuperating from the physical changes of pregnancy and childbirth and, quite likely, nursing as well.

The following comments about fatigue are therefore directed

to you as the mother. They are, however, in no way intended to overlook the importance of fathers in rearing small children, nor to slight those fathers who are carrying the primary child-care load, whether married or single. We hope they, too, will find this material useful.

Mothers who stay at home with one or more kids under the age of three may find themselves suffering from lack of sleep, lack of adult conversation, and (most important) lack of recognition for the job being done. All of these can sap huge amounts of energy from the most talented, motivated, and dedicated moms.

If you are in this position, you may begin to suspect that the only milestones in your life are those achieved by your children and that you are a fool for staying home while your childless friends are busy earning advanced degrees or accomplishing great things in their glamorous careers.

If you feel that there is no end to your day's work and that life has been reduced to an endless, draining, and monotonous routine, wake up and smell the coffee, because life is not passing you by. On the contrary, you are at the center of the action. You are shaping and molding the very core—the attitudes, the faith, the future—of one or more young lives. *Very few careers offer anything resembling this opportunity and none to the depth that is possible as a parent.* Believe it or not, your friends who are navigating the freeways by the dawn's early light may actually envy you.

This is a time to renew your fascination with your child and to remind yourself that you have him on loan for but a few short years. An attitude of deep thanksgiving—even in the midst of toys strewn all over the house, piles of laundry yet to be done, crayon marks on the walls, and little hands frequently pulling at your sleeve—is not only appropriate but invigorating.

While it may seem as if the current responsibilities will last forever, there will in fact be many years ahead to pursue education and career, if that's your calling. Who said that you had to check your mind at the door of the maternity ward or that your reading must forever be limited to *The Runaway Bunny* or *The Cat in the Hat*? There is no law against ongoing learning while children are young, whether through informal study or more formal courses (even one at a time) taken at a local college or other continuing-education resource.

The arrival of your child's second birthday is also an important time to take stock of the parental state of the union. Is there still a strong sense of teamwork, shared goals, communication, and intimacy? Or are Mom and Dad moving through the months on different tracks, which may be parallel but more likely are diverging? Without taking deliberate steps to maintain your marriage, drifting in different directions is all too easy. Both husband and wife must take part in keeping their marriage fresh and strong.

As important as it is to maintain communication within your marriage, your spouse may not be able to meet all your needs in this area. Regular times of grown-up conversation with other adults of the same gender who share your values can help keep the demands of each day in perspective.

Time-outs for personal refreshment—not just for running errands but for exercise, coffee with a friend, an unscheduled afternoon out, or time to be alone with God—are both legitimate and necessary. Track down the best babysitters in your area and reward them well. If cash is short, consider utilizing a babysitting co-op with people you know well, where child care is swapped among several people on a barter system. If you are blessed with loving grandparents nearby, give them the opportunity to spoil the kids for a few hours (or even overnight) while you take a break.

Mothers who work outside of the home, whether single or married, face additional generators of pressure and fatigue. Fulfilling the responsibilities of a job requires that the demands and details of parenting be carried out during fewer hours—often at the end of a workday when a great deal of energy has already been expended. You may feel guilt ridden over the time you have to be away at work or concerned about the adequacy of your day-care arrangements ("Are they doing as good a job as I would?"). Worries over income, especially for single moms, may add to the burden.

All these issues might tempt you to abandon reasonable lim-its that your child needs or to spend money you don't have to make up for any shortages in your time and attention. Whatever you do, don't allow a child to play the guilt card in order to get his way or con you into buying something for him. *Remember that consistency in expressing love and enforcing reasonable limits is far more valuable to your child in the long run than a lot of mate-rial goods.*

If both parents work outside of the home, cooperation, commu-nication, and sharing responsibilities will be even more impor-tant. The suggestions already listed for homes in which one parent (usually the mother) is at home definitely apply to you as well, with slight modification.

Single parents have the challenging and important job of being both mother and father to their children and creating an environment for them that is safe and stable. If you are a single parent, you may at times wonder whether you can really carry out all these obligations adequately, especially if hours are long and income is limited. The answer is that you can, especially if you stay with the basics: love and limits for your children, lots of prayer, and a little help from your friends. As mentioned in previous chapters, you should maintain and tap into your sup-port team (family, friends, church groups, pregnancy resource centers) for ongoing camaraderie, attitude adjustment, trouble-shooting, and adult conversation. Maintain a stable attitude with your children, and in future years they will rise up and bless you, marveling at what you accomplished without a mate.

How can I encourage my husband to step up and provide the help I need with our two-year-old?

A mom who's been home all day with her kids needs two primary things from her husband: (a) an adult pair of hands to pitch in, and (b) adult conversation, including expressions of appreciation for what she has been doing.

If you feel that you are not getting what you need from your husband, talk with him! First, consider the list below to help you figure out what exactly you need from him. How would you complete the following sentence? My husband could help me most by:

- Taking charge of one or more kids at the end of the day, so that I could have a brief (thirty- to sixty-minute) time-out from child-care responsibilities.

- Wrangling dirty diapers or picking up other debris around the home.

- Getting involved in or even taking over the process of getting our kids ready for bed.

- Taking on one or more tasks at home—preparing meals or doing laundry, for example—that would lighten my load when I'm feeling exhausted.

- Picking up his own clothes and possessions.

- Asking me about my day and then filling me in on his.

- Calling me during the day to touch base, offer an encouraging word, or simply say "I love you."

- Maintaining the habit of a regular date night—a meal (fancy or otherwise), a walk, a concert, whatever our imagination and budget can manage—in which the focus is on conversation and companionship.

- Reining in the hours he spends at work—especially if his long days/nights are gradually turning me into a single parent—and letting me know whenever he is going to be later than expected.

- Taking me away for a romantic weekend, or even just dinner and an overnight stay, at a pleasant location where my daily responsibilities are temporarily suspended.

- Understanding that, like virtually all young moms, I may not have much (or any) sexual drive at this phase of my life—especially if I'm exhausted and feeling disconnected from him—but that my sexual response will be rekindled by meaningful conversation, compliments, acts of kindness, and some elbow grease applied to helping reduce my to-do list.

After you are clear on how he could help you most, choose a time when you're both relaxed (in other words, not two minutes after he arrives home from work or just after you've spent thirty minutes calming a screaming child) to discuss how he might lighten your load.

Be sure to start by affirming him for what he is already doing and acknowledging his own long list of concerns and responsibilities. The reality is that you both have tiring days and ideally your requests shouldn't be perceived as a complaint list. Ask him if there is anything you could do to help him foster his bonds with your child. Above all, let him know that your relationship with him is still a top priority for you, even when one or more small children require so much of your time and attention.

CHAPTER 7

●●● THREE- AND FOUR-YEAR-OLDS

AN EXTRAORDINARY PERIOD awaits you during the next months as baby days and toddlerhood become more distant memories. For many reasons, the next two years leading to the fifth birthday are a unique and critical period during which you can shape the gamut of your child's attitudes and understanding.

Developments in his intellect and speech will enable you to communicate with him in much more sophisticated ways. He will still be intensely curious about the world around him and is now better equipped to learn about it. More important, he will also want to understand how *you* see things both great and small and what is important to you. Whether the topic is animals, trucks, the color of the sky, or the attributes of God, he will be all ears (even though his mouth may seem to be in perpetual motion) and deeply concerned about what you think.

What physical developments should I expect in my three- or four-year-old?

During the next twenty-four months, your child's growth should maintain a steady, if not spectacular, pace. You can expect gains of two and a half to three inches (6.3 to 7.6 cm) and four to five pounds (1.8 to 2.3 kg) each year. He will continue his gradual physical transition from toddler to child: More baby fat will disappear, his abdomen will no longer protrude, and his arms and legs will slim down so they look almost scrawny. Don't be too concerned if his limbs look a bit delicate, since muscle development will catch up in due time. Indeed, if a chunky look persists well past the third birthday, ask his health-care provider to check how he's doing on the height and weight chart. (By the way, the flat foot you saw when he was a toddler should be developing an arch.)

His walking, running, and jumping movements should become increasingly smooth and will be joined by tiptoeing, hopping, spinning, and standing on one foot. By age four he will also climb up and down stairs without holding a rail or your hand. He will enjoy pedaling a tricycle and throwing a ball, although his ability to catch a ball with any reliability will develop somewhat later. He will, however, be thrilled if he succeeds in snagging any soft object that you gently toss right to him. If you take him to a local park, he will relish his time on small-scale swings, slides, and climbing gear and in tunnels and sandboxes.

Although he won't career randomly from one place to another as he did as a toddler, don't be surprised when he charges ahead of you in the park, church, mall—or at the end of the sidewalk. At this age enthusiasm and the desire for independence are far more abundant than are wisdom and judgment. Keep your eyes peeled and a good grip on your child's hand when you are approaching traffic, playing near a pool, or walking through a crowd.

You'll notice your child's fine motor skills advancing in these years as well. When drawing with a pencil or crayon, he will begin to use a more sophisticated grip, with thumb on one side and fingers on the other, rather than grasping with his fist. Watch for his first wonderful drawing of a person—with arms and legs extending directly from the head. After he turns four, his "people pictures" will begin to include details such as facial features (eyes, nose, ears) and eventually a body to which the arms and legs are attached. When not creating his own images on paper, he may enjoy tracing or reproducing geometric shapes.

Budding young artists also delight in using brushes, clay, paste, and finger paints—materials that are much more fun for everyone if clothes, furniture, and carpets aren't in jeopardy. Wearing grubby clothes and setting up shop in the yard (or laying down lots of newspaper indoors) is a good idea. Kid-safe, blunt-ended scissors are also a big hit with this age-group, but be sure everyone is clear on what is to be cut and what is to be left alone.

Your child will also develop new skills manipulating other types of objects: jigsaw puzzles with a few pieces, fasteners and buttons for his own or his toys' clothes, and building blocks, among other things. Meals should generate less cleanup as he becomes more adept at using his fork and spoon. Since some accidents and spills are inevitable, you may want to wait another couple of years before adding glassware to his dining equipment.

How can I help my child's language development?

Your child arrived at his third birthday with a vocabulary of about five hundred to one thousand words. During the next two years, you can anticipate a dramatic increase to about twenty-five hundred words. At age three, these will be gathered into sentences of five or six words, and from here on the assembly of words into phrases and sentences will gradually become more sophisticated.

In the coming years, your child will begin revealing his ideas, his rhymes and music, his fantasies, his questions, and his fears.

Language will be a window into his soul and spirit—and the most obvious evidence that you are dealing with a unique human being.

He will soon be using personal pronouns (*I*, *you*, *he*, *she*), and you can speed up his process of sorting them out by using them correctly yourself. As natural as it may seem to refer to yourself and your child in the third person ("Mommy wants Andrew to get into the tub"), this is the time to begin using the words *I* and *you* instead. When he mixes them up ("Me want a cookie"), be careful that your correction doesn't create further confusion. (If you say, "You mean, '*I want a cookie*,'" he may think that you want one too. A correction such as "Andrew, you should say, '*I want a cookie*'" would work better.)

Pronouns won't be the only verbal mistakes you will hear. Other mispronunciations will be abundant, although you (or anyone else) should be able to understand what he is trying to say. Your friends should not need an interpreter when he speaks; if he is truly unintelligible at this age, he should have a formal speech evaluation.

What can I do to help my child develop her language skills?

You can take several steps to help your child's language blossom:

- **Read to her and with her.** Now is a great time to begin going to the library regularly.

- **Listen.** Take the time occasionally to stop what you're doing, look into her eyes, and acknowledge what she says. ("Wow! That's pretty exciting! What else happened?")

- **Carry on conversations.** In addition to listening, begin engaging in thoughtful exchanges. It's amazing how much you'll learn simply by talking with your child without scolding, exhorting, or correcting.

- **Try to answer her questions.** You'll hear them from dawn till dusk, and if you can give a simple but meaningful answer, not a mumbled "I dunno" or a disinterested shrug, your child will learn language, information, and values. At this age, she cares very much what you think about life and the world, a state that won't last forever.

What should I do if my child stutters?

One common language glitch at this age is stuttering or stammering, which may cause some concern when you first hear it. Before you call a speech therapist, however, understand that one in twenty preschool children manifests this on a temporary basis, especially when tired, excited, or upset. Boys are three times more likely to stutter than girls. This may be a case of too many words in the assembly line between the thought and the actual expression. The opening syllable or even the first couple of words in a sentence may trip repeatedly on the tongue before moving on to the rest of the thought. "Um" or "uh" may show up midword or midsentence if he loses track of where the idea was going.

Don't worry about this if it occurs on an occasional basis over a month or so. Avoid showing impatience or disapproval while he's trying to get through his sentence. Also, don't try to fish the words out for him, complete his thoughts, or add any pressure to the situation. If anything, his stuttering may be a signal that the speed and pitch of everyone's conversation at home needs to calm down a bit. Normally this situation will resolve itself. However, if your child is having an ongoing problem getting his sentences launched, looks tense, twitches and grimaces, or is definitely upset by his stuttering, he should be evaluated by a speech therapist.

How will my child continue to develop socially?

You will probably note several themes in his play and social interactions during this stage:

Mimicry and imitation. While this generally begins at age two, it becomes more obvious during the preschool years. If you are working in the garden, your son will want to dig and rake along with you. If you're sorting laundry, he may be surprisingly good at finding the matching socks. If you're setting the table, he is quite capable of learning what goes where and eventually can carry out this everyday task on his own.

Try not to look at his efforts to participate as a hassle that will bog you down. Rather, see them as giving you an opportunity to chat with him during everyday activities and giving him practice in some basic skills in the process. Not only does he need your praise and affirmation for wanting to help, but it is healthy for him to experience the act of serving someone else, even if his attention span is rather short.

Don't forget that imitation can include negative behaviors as well. If you hit your finger with a hammer, guess who will learn some new words if you don't watch how you react. If you use harsh words when there's a disagreement, guess who is learning a non-productive way to solve problems. If you slam your fist on the table when you become frustrated, guess who will be scared or do the same thing when he feels the same way.

What may be a little frustrating during this stage is that you may hear him mimic the words and tone of voice that you use when you're blowing off steam, yet not see a whole lot of evidence that he is imitating your positive role modeling.

Before you become discouraged, keep two facts in mind. First, your child really *is* taking in the flavor of your habits and conversations at home. They form the foundation of his expectations and assumptions about life: what he is used to, what he considers normal, what he will carry with him throughout his life (including the family he starts himself in another twenty or thirty years). Believe it or not, your attitudes are being caught.

Second, a healthy and wholesome family environment does

not override the core of self-centeredness that is present in every human being from birth. The manifestations of willfulness and negativity that you saw in your child as a toddler and a two-year-old probably have been contained by now, but they sprang from deep roots that never completely disappear. Therefore, you need to not only demonstrate virtues but teach them as well. Saying please and thank you (and later understanding a depth of meaning in these words), waiting one's turn, and telling the truth need to not only be observed but also talked about and practiced on an ongoing basis.

Role-playing and fantasy. This staple activity of childhood will get into full swing during the preschool years. Whether in your home, at a play group, or among other children in the neighborhood, you can bet the children will play variations on "let's pretend" with great fervor.

In general, this is not only normal but healthy. Pretending to be Moses or Cinderella, setting up a store or a ranch on the back patio, and devising their own adventures will exercise language and the imagination far more than staring at a TV screen. Children can learn to plan, solve problems, and cooperate with one another during these projects. In fact, your child(ren) will be ecstatic if you occasionally enter into the adventure yourself.

You can generally allow these make-believe sessions to proceed with a minimum of parental intrusion, but keep your eyes and ears open for a few situations that might need some revision of the script:

- *Inappropriate characters.* While someone may want to play Captain Hook or Goliath to round out the characters in a make-believe story, role-playing options shouldn't include serial killers, vampires, or other relentless evildoers. Suggest more heroic or more neutral characters.

- *Destructive scenarios.* Action and conflict drive many adventures, from knights in armor to Wild West and outer-space fantasies. But if your child's pretend characters do nothing but ninja-kick, wave laser sabers, fire toy guns, and generally inflict make-believe (if not real) damage, you may want to suggest some less violent alternatives.

- *Toxic fantasy.* This is a tough call in some cases because fantasy elements of many stories (such as C. S. Lewis's Chronicles of Narnia) can serve to convey some very positive values. But role-playing that involves "pretend" occult practices (such as séances or Ouija boards) or elaborate spell casting could whet young appetites for more hazardous practices later on.

- *Hurt feelings.* When the pretending is orchestrated by older children, younger or less popular participants may become stuck with roles no one else wants or receive lots of "make-believe" abuse that starts to feel like the real thing. If someone regularly seems to be getting the short end of the stick, suggest alternative casting as well as caution about the kinds of things that are said, even when pretending.

- *Too much of a good thing.* Preschoolers can become so enthused about pretending to be Superman or Pocahontas that they may not want the game to end, or they may try to use their character to gain power or attention. When your call to get into the tub is met with a resounding refusal ("X-wing pilots don't need baths!"), you'll have to decide whether to have your way by playing along ("Your bath orders come directly from your squadron leader!") or by calling for an intermission.

- *Early adolescence.* Little girls love to play "lady dress up" with old hats, costume jewelry, and gloves. However, if your

four-year-old insists on putting on nail polish and frilly
dresses for every occasion or becomes overly infatuated
with the teenage social life of a popular doll, you might
encourage her to broaden her horizons.

Making friends. Preschoolers are usually ready for some genuine
cooperative play. The concepts of sharing and taking turns can
now be understood and usually put into action, but reminders and
supervision will still be necessary.

Some children enter a bossy phase during this period, which
can make things unpleasant for younger or less assertive children
in their vicinity. If your child begins to sound like a miniature dic-
tator, take her aside for a gentle reminder about basic kindness
and manners. Also be sure to give her lots of praise when she plays
well with other children. Specific information helps: "I like the
way you let Megan have the ball so nicely when she asked for it."

Along with the make-believe and role-playing activities, your
child will begin enjoying a variety of interactions with other children, such as simple games, puzzles, and creating buildings and
roads with blocks and other construction toys.

What should I expect at mealtimes?

During the coming months, your child will continue to show wide
variations in her desire for food. A ravenous appetite one day followed by picking and dawdling sessions the next won't be at all
unusual. Just as when she was two, your job will be to provide
an appropriate mix of healthy options; her job will be to decide
how much of each (within reason) she will consume. If you need a
calorie estimate of her needs, figure about forty calories per pound
(or about ninety calories per kilogram) per day. A child weighing thirty-five pounds (about 16 kg), for example, will consume
about fourteen hundred calories per day, spread over three meals
and two snacks. Between 25 and 35 percent of the total calories

should be in the form of fats. Milk should be kept to a maximum of sixteen ounces (about 475 ml) per day. Vitamin supplements are not necessary at this age, but if you have any concerns, check with your doctor.

In the coming months, you will want to pay more attention to the patterns of your child's food intake than to the details of what she eats at any particular meal. Specifically, keep the following in mind:

- Emphasize variety and freshness.

- Resist the encroachment of sugary, salty, fatty, and otherwise low-quality enticements.

- Don't use food as a distraction or as a way to make your child feel better. It should not become a cure for boredom, a pacifier for a stubbed toe, or a bribe for doing something you want.

It's also critically important at this age not to allow meals to turn into power struggles. If you provide a wholesome selection of foods at a meal and she isn't interested, don't fight over it, make it the main subject of conversation, or force her to sit for hours at the table until she eats it. Put her plate in the refrigerator, and take it out again when she's hungry. Don't be badgered into preparing something specifically for her at every meal, and don't allow her to become stuck in a rut of three or four foods that are "the only things she ever eats." She won't starve if you hold your ground.

While busy schedules may rule out formal dining three times a day, at least one meal a day should pull the family around the table at the same time. Dinner is most often the choice, but for many children breakfast is the biggest meal of the day, and socializing at that time may be more productive than at other times. For some families, one or two meals per week—perhaps Saturday breakfast or Sunday dinner after church—serve as the special time everyone can come together. At such times, the atmosphere should be relaxed and inviting. The TV should be off, phones silenced, and conversation geared to draw everyone into this important event.

A preschooler is old enough to learn some basic table manners: keeping the volume of her voice reasonable, chewing with her mouth closed, saying please and thank you, using a napkin, and waiting until everyone is seated and a blessing is offered before beginning to eat. If she is done with her meal and conversation among the adults is extending beyond her interest and attention span, don't insist that she sit indefinitely. But before she gets up, she should ask to be excused. After she departs, don't let her crawl around under the table with the family pets.

What should I keep in mind when planning playdates for my child?

During your child's preschool years, she will probably begin asking to invite a friend over for playtime or a meal, and she will most likely receive a similar invitation in return. You should already have some idea of the ground rules of the other family, and vice versa, before this "cultural exchange" takes place. Obviously, your child can't live in a glass bubble, but it would be desirable if the basic standards and values you hold dear aren't undermined by playmates at this young age. If she brings home words or attitudes from a friend's house that rub you the wrong way, talk to her about what you find troublesome, and then see if you can influence the other child and her family in a more positive direction. If you can't make any headway with a playmate who is having a negative impact on your child, you may need to direct your child's attention to other children.

Where can you find prospective companions for your preschooler? If your circle of friends or immediate neighborhood doesn't include any families with children the same age, check the ranks of your church. Assuming child care is provided, you might see if she hits it off with someone while you're attending the service.

You may wish to enroll your child in a preschool or other structured playgroup for a specified amount of time each week. While the term *preschooler* is used widely as a synonym for a three- or four-year-old child, whether your child actually attends preschool is completely up to you. This experience is not a requirement for future academic achievement or necessary for proper social development. If she's ready, she'll enjoy it, and you may find the break in child care a welcome change of pace during the week.

In what other ways will my child begin to exert some independence during these years?

You may have to deal with peer pressure for the first time as your child's social skills and interests in other children begin to blossom. A child who normally is cautious about taking risks may suddenly decide he wants to climb on, jump off, or crawl under something that is off-limits—in response to the tempting, teasing, encouragement, or example of other children. As a result, during the coming months you will need to begin teaching your child, in very simple terms, the "why" of your rules, along with the "what and where" (or more often the "what not" and "where not").

At this age it is likely that he will push you a little or even wear you out with "Why . . . ?" questions. This isn't necessarily an attempt to start an argument but more likely a sign of growth and simple curiosity about the "whys" in his world—including your limits and ground rules. Try to use the reason "Because I'm the mom, that's why!" sparingly. You are now building your child's value system, precept upon precept, as well as his ability to link actions with consequences. At this age, he is beginning to understand and is capable of appreciating the reasons for your rules. Take advantage of his openness by explaining them whenever you can.

How can I encourage my child to follow my directions without whining or arguing?

Ideally your child should respond to specific directions ("Please pick up your toys now") without delay, distraction, or argument. In reality, many parents would faint if their child actually obeyed them right away without fussing or complaining. By putting the following principles into action, it's not as unreasonable a goal as it might seem: (1) When appropriate, give a little advance notice if you intend to interrupt something your child is doing; (2) if and when your child doesn't do what you've asked, take action and explain why without getting angry or raising your voice; (3) make certain that you respond to your child's misbehavior promptly; and (4) be sure to enforce your rules and limits *consistently*.

My child has discovered his private parts. What should I do?

During or before toddler days, your child undoubtedly discovered that touching the genital area felt good, and you may have been dismayed to see little hands exploring inside the diaper zone (whether clean or otherwise) on a number of occasions. This type of exploration and ongoing curiosity about body parts is common and quite normal in young children. Questions about where they (or their siblings) came from are part of the same package. When it comes to dealing with such sensitive areas and topics, you have a number of important assignments:

Make it clear that you are the prime source of information about these matters—and not the kid next door or some other unreliable source. Be levelheaded, honest, calm, and straightforward when you name body parts and explain what they do. Using actual terms (penis and vagina) and not more colorful vocabulary may save some embarrassment later on if your child happens to make a public pronouncement. This information by itself doesn't jeopardize your child's innocence.

Instill respect for the body your child has been given, the Creator who made it, and the functions it performs. This means that you should not communicate a sense of shame or repulsion about any part of your child's (or your own) anatomy. It also means that you need to teach what, where, when, and how it is appropriate to touch or talk about these areas.

Your child needs to know that these are things to discuss at home with Mom and/or Dad and not with other kids in the neighborhood. If you discover him and a playmate checking out each other's pelvic area, don't panic. This is also normal curiosity at work, and he just needs a brushup on the ground rules. Remind him that these areas of his body are just for himself, his parents, and his doctor to see, and not other people. Tell your child that if someone else tries to touch those areas, he should protest noisily, get away, and tell you as soon as possible. He must know that you will not be angry or upset with him if this should happen.

If a child makes comments, gestures, or body movements that suggest exposure to or experience with sexual activity, further evaluation will be needed. Other signs of possible sexual abuse include age-inappropriate sexual behavior or demonstrations, depression, disturbed sleep, fear of being left alone, or pain on urination. You will need to review what you have seen and heard with your physician, who will investigate and/or refer you to an appropriate professional for further evaluation.

Release information on a need-to-know basis. Your child does not need to hear everything about reproduction in one sitting and will be overwhelmed (or bored) if you try to explain too much at once.

THREE- AND FOUR-YEAR-OLDS ●●● 177

How do I respond when my child uses inappropriate language?

If your child cuts loose with offensive language that he didn't hear from you, stay calm and respond forthrightly with a minimum of fluster. It is unlikely that he even understands what he just said, as a simple quiz ("Do you know what that means?") will often confirm. He is far more likely to be interested in the power of words to create a stir than in actually expressing some specific sexual or crude sentiment. Without sounding alarmed or flustered, explain that the words he just used are not ones that you use in your family and that he needs to stop saying them in your home or anywhere else. You should emphasize that such words and expressions put down other people and can make them feel upset or even afraid.

If your child's new expressions include casual or inappropriate use of the words *God* or *Jesus*, a simple explanation about the importance of respecting those names will be needed as well.

Once you have stated your case, be sure to take appropriate action if you hear a repeat performance. If he persists after one or two reminders, let him know that a consequence will follow next time, and then carry it out if needed. If your child begins using harsh or obscene language, you need to not only retrain his vocabulary quickly and decisively but also have a frank conversation with whomever you determine to be the source.

How important is a car seat at this age?

Car seats are still necessary for children this age; keep in mind that *adult seat belts are not designed for children in this age-group*. Every time your child rides in a car, he should be secured in a child safety seat with a full harness. When he reaches the weight limit of the seat (typically forty pounds, or 18.2 kg), he can graduate to a booster seat. He won't be ready for regular lap and shoulder belts until he is about eight years old, or at least four feet nine inches tall (fifty-seven inches, or 145 cm).

Now that my child is almost potty trained, what should I expect?

By the third birthday or soon thereafter, it is likely that your child will be well versed in the basics of using the toilet. If you are still working through this process, review the previous chapter.

Your next assignment in this area will be to teach the skills necessary for solo trips to the toilet, which will be desirable if preschool is on the horizon and necessary for kindergarten. These skills include:

- Learning how to get clothes and underwear out of the way and then reassembled afterward. Obviously, easy-on, easy-off garments are desirable. Boys at this age are still a little young for zippers, which have a way of getting stuck or (worse) accidentally pinching the penis when zipped up.

- Learning how to wipe clean after a bowel movement. Girls need to be taught to wipe front to back to reduce the risk of moving bacteria from the anus to the opening of the vagina and bladder, where the bacteria can gain access to the bladder and start an infection.

- Learning to finish the job by flushing and then washing hands with soap.

- For little boys, learning to urinate standing up.

- Learning to use restrooms out of the house. You'll need to give directions during visits to public facilities, pointing out things of interest such as the appropriate gender sign on the restroom door, the flush handle (if it's different from the ones at home), faucets/paper towels/hand dryers, and so on. (Even after these skills are well established, you should continue to escort your child on any trip to a public restroom. At this age he is by no means ready to handle a chance encounter with someone whose behavior might be inappropriate or abusive.)

What should I do if my child is still wetting the bed?

Your child may not be waking up dry in the morning at this point. In fact, by the age of five, at least 10 to 20 percent of children occasionally or regularly wet the bed. For some children this problem persists for years, and often in such cases there is a family history of this problem. *Rewards, (or worse) reprimands, humiliation, and punishment have no place in dealing with bed-wetting because the problem is one of physiological maturity and is completely out of a child's control.* The best solution in nearly all cases is patience, continued use of diapers or training pants to contain the nocturnal flood, a lot of reassurance, and a few more birthdays.

If your child has been dry through the night for a number of months and then begins to lose bladder control, a physical problem such as a bladder infection or an emotional upheaval such as a move or a new sibling might be the cause. A visit to the doctor would be a good idea if this occurs.

Will my child's sleeping routine change at this age?

Most three- and four-year-olds will sleep about twelve hours each night. A daytime nap may continue to be part of your child's routine, but don't be surprised when it is phased out during the next several months. If you are struggling with your child over bedtime, see pages 151–155 for some tips. This is also a good time to review the management of nightmares (and their less common counterparts, night terrors) described in that same section.

Remember that bedtime should be early because your child needs the sleep and you need time with other children, your spouse, or yourself. You will need to decide how much to bend your routines to match the seasons, or perhaps invest in heavy window shades if you need to darken your child's room in the summer when we enjoy more hours of sunlight. You may also need to exercise sensible flexibility to accommodate family work schedules.

The activities that surround getting tucked in should become a familiar and quieting routine. At this age, bedtime can be a delightful, enlightening experience. You can introduce your child to some wonderful stories, including books with several chapters that can create eager anticipation for the next night's installment ("I wonder what's going to happen to Pooh and Piglet tonight. Better get ready for bed so we can find out!"). Your child's desire to keep the lights on and you in the room as long as possible will usually cause her to be remarkably transparent and receptive.

You will also need to deal with some childhood fears when it's time to tuck in. Monsters in the closet, under the bed, or outside the window may need to be banished. Be sure to ask what your child has in mind—is the creature something from a book or video, or perhaps a tall tale spun by an insensitive adolescent next door? Are there tensions at home creating a need for reassurance?

Very often the beast in question doesn't exist except in someone's imagination. In this case it can be tempting to give a lighthearted, direct inspection ("I don't see any monsters in your closet—just a lot of junk!"), but you may leave the impression that there are monsters or aliens running around *somewhere*—they just don't happen to be here at the moment. For these fears, more decisive reality checks are important ("Bigfoot isn't under your bed or anywhere else").

When the issue is burglars or other villains who actually *do* exist out there, you will need to be more specific about the safeguards in your home: You are present (or if you are going out, someone you trust will be there), the doors are locked, and perhaps you have a dog or an alarm system that adds to your home's security. In addition, remind your child that God is keeping watch over her twenty-four hours a day. What your child really wants is reassurance and confidence that things are under control.

If a fearful bedtime resistance persists or escalates, take time to find out if something else is bothering her. Did your child see a disturbing image on TV or a video? Did she hear an argument the other night? Did something else frighten her? Once you have spent time exploring the problem, it's okay to make some minor adjustments to reduce the anxiety level: leaving a light on in the hallway or the door open a little wider, for example. But don't get pulled into more elaborate or manipulative routines, such as her insisting on falling asleep in your bed or on the living-room floor when she claims that she's afraid of something. She needs to know that she will be just as safe and sound in her own bed as anywhere else.

What should I expect at my child's medical checkups during these two years?

Your child's medical checkups at ages three and four will probably be rather uneventful, but he shouldn't skip them. Aside from checking growth and developmental milestones and giving a head-to-toe exam, his health-care provider may recommend giving him his DTaP (diphtheria/tetanus/pertussis) and polio boosters if he has passed his fourth birthday. He will probably also receive his second dose of MMR (measles/mumps/rubella) vaccine between ages four and six. Yearly influenza vaccines will be given in the fall, and a series of immunizations to protect against hepatitis A may also be recommended during these visits.

How can I encourage my child's spiritual development at this age?

Don't buy into the idea that your child's spiritual development is such a personal matter that you should make no attempt to influence the direction the child chooses. While your child must ultimately decide on her own whether or not she will begin and nurture a relationship with God, you have not only an opportunity but a responsibility to teach and demonstrate the spiritual principles that are the foundation of your family life.

So how do you communicate spiritual truths and moral values to a three- or four-year-old? Can she conceive of an infinite God or understand theology or sit through a religious service? Both Old and New Testaments address this quite plainly:

> Hear, O Israel: The LORD our God, the LORD is one. Love the LORD your God with all your heart and with all your soul and with all your strength. These commandments that I give you today are to be upon your hearts. Impress them on your children. Talk about them when you sit at home and when you walk along the road, when you lie down and when you get up. Tie them as symbols on your hands and bind them on your foreheads. Write them on the doorframes of your houses and on your gates.
> (DEUTERONOMY 6:4-9)

> Jesus called the children to him and said, "Let the little children come to me, and do not hinder them, for the kingdom of God belongs to such as these. I tell you the truth, anyone who will not receive the kingdom of God like a little child will never enter it."
> (LUKE 18:16-17)

First, we are to talk to our children about God as we go about our daily business. As important as regular observances can and should be, spiritual matters shouldn't be confined to a specified religious time slot once a week. Conversations about God should be as routine and natural as those about any other subject. Our children should see us pray about the issues of our lives, give thanks for our food (and everything else), and acknowledge God's leadership in our decisions. In dealing with more formal teaching or family devotions, simple stories will communicate volumes to preschoolers. The Scriptures are filled with them, and Jesus often told stories to get His point across.

Second, small children appear uniquely qualified to understand intimacy with God in ways that may elude them later in life. Perhaps it is their utter trust in their earthly parents (which can be expanded to include a heavenly Father), their lack of cynicism, their openness, or their uninhibited joy and enthusiasm for the objects of their love that draw them to the God they cannot see. Whatever else parents and the other adults who care for children do, they must not hinder children from trusting in God, which seems to come naturally to them.

One important job for parents who care about the spiritual lives of their preschoolers is to help them distinguish not only right from wrong but truth from fantasy. This means that you will have to make some careful decisions about dealing with a few popular traditions in our culture. The crux of the matter is this: If your child is going to take you seriously when you talk about the God who made heaven and earth, you don't have the luxury of deliberately bending the truth (or tying it in knots) in other matters. Whatever else you do, never mislead your child when she asks you point-blank for the facts about mythical personalities or anything else.

On a day-to-day basis, you will also have a responsibility to help your preschooler understand the difference between truth and make-believe in her own life. At an age when there is so much to learn about the world and so much imagination at work in your child's head, the boundaries between reality and fantasy will wear thin at times. If you hear a breathless report that there are giant spiders crawling around her room, and it appears that her main interest is in gathering attention or reassurance, explain what can go wrong if she makes up alarming stories. A brief recounting of the fate of the boy who cried wolf may be in order.

If she tells a whopper of a tale to explain why her dollhouse is now caved in on one side ("A big gorilla climbed through my window and jumped on it!"), you will need to coax the truth out with some finesse. In particular, she must understand that telling a lie to escape punishment is far more of a concern than the actual misdeed itself. The first offense in this area should be treated more with explanation than with punishment, but repeated episodes will require specific and meaningful consequences. Otherwise a habit of lying will eventually undermine every relationship in her life.

You cannot afford to demonstrate any "white lies" of your own. If your child hears you say, "Tell him I'm not here" when an obnoxious caller is on the phone, for example, whatever you are trying to teach about truth and lies will be wasted breath.

This is an appropriate time to present your child with her own Bible (age appropriate and containing lots of pictures), which can provide a rich source of input and topics for conversation. Tell her stories of Old and New Testament heroes, and above all, talk about the life and deeds of Jesus again and again. Should your preschooler memorize Scripture? Some are able to commit Bible verses to memory quite easily before their fifth birthday, and for these children the words will be "hidden in their hearts" for the rest of their lives. For others, attempts to memorize are like pulling teeth, and if you force the issue, you may create a distaste for Scripture rivaling that for their least favorite foods.

A more effective way to hide the Word in a child's heart when she doesn't memorize easily is to use songs. Many CDs and DVDs communicate spiritual principles and Scripture verses to children (and their parents) through music. The best of these not only teach and entertain but leave both parent and child humming uplifting tunes—sometimes for years to come. Few investments pay such rich dividends.

●●● Notes

1. Carol L. Wagner, M.D., Frank R. Greer, M.D., and the Section on Breastfeeding and Committee on Nutrition, "Clinical Report: Prevention of Rickets and Vitamin D Deficiency in Infants, Children, and Adolescents," *Pediatrics* 122, no. 2 (November 2008): 1142–1152 (doi:10.1542/peds.2008-1862). http://aappolicy.aappublications.org /cgi/content/full/pediatrics;122/5/1142.
2. American Academy of Pediatrics, "Policy Statement: Breastfeeding and the Use of Human Milk," *Pediatrics* 115, no. 2 (February 2005): 496–506, http://aappolicy.aappublications.org/cgi/content/full /pediatrics;115/2/496.
3. Ibid.
4. Isadora B. Stehlin, "Infant Formula: Second Best but Good Enough," *FDA Consumer Magazine* (June 1996), http://babyparenting.about .com/cs/formulafeeding/a/formula.htm; AskDr.Sears.com, "Sterilizing," http://www.askdrsears.com/topics/feeding-infants-toddlers /bottle-feeding/sterilizing.
5. National Institute of Child Health and Human Development, Health Information and Media, "Infant Sleep Position and SIDS: Questions and Answers for Health Care Providers," June 2007, http://www.nichd.nih .gov/publications/pubs/upload/SIDS_QA-508-rev.pdf.
6. Consumer Product Safety Commission, "CPSC Cautions Caregivers about Hidden Hazards for Babies on Adult Beds: Reports of More Than 100 Deaths from 1999–2001," http://www.cpsc.gov/CPSCPUB/PUBS /5091.html.
7. Jonathan Eig, "Sippy Cups Draw Fire for Speech Slurs, Cavities," *Wall Street Journal*, February 12, 2002, http://www.mindfully.org/Plastic /Sippy-Cups-Slur-Speech12feb02.htm.

8. Centers for Disease Control and Prevention, "Insect Repellent Use and Safety," August 2005, http://www.cdc.gov/ncidod/dvbid/westnile/qa/insect_repellent.htm.

9. US Food and Drug Administration, "Insect Repellent Use and Safety in Children," January 2010, http://www.fda.gov/Drugs>/Emergency Preparedness/ucm085277.htm.

●●● Index

About the Author

DR. PAUL REISSER is a family physician in Southern California. He has been a member of Focus on the Family's Physicians Resource Council since 1991, and he served as the primary author of Focus on the Family's *Complete Guide to Baby and Child Care*. He married Teri, a marriage and family therapist, in 1975 and is still very happy about that decision. They have two grown children, three wonderful grandchildren, and one lovable but spoiled dog.

Look for these additional parenting resources wherever fine books are sold:

Complete Guide to Baby & Child Care is a comprehensive guidebook to parenting from before birth through the end of the teen years. It takes a balanced, commonsense approach to raising children to be healthy emotionally, physically, mentally, and spiritually. This indispensable guide delivers practical and critical information parents need to know, including 25 Special Concerns sections that cover topics such as fever in small children, effective discipline, ADHD, cyberspace safety, and much more!

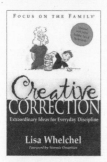

Creative Correction
Drawing from her own family's experiences and from interaction with other parents, Lisa Whelchel offers creative solutions for parents who are out of ideas and desperate for new, proven approaches to discipline. In addition to advice on topics such as sibling conflict and lying, Whelchel offers a biblical perspective and down-to-earth encouragement for parents who are feeling overwhelmed.

Essentials of Parenting
Becoming a parent is one of God's greatest gifts in life. Children don't, however, come with an instruction manual, so where can parents turn to get the answers they need? Essentials of Parenting™ DVD series brings top childrearing experts into your home or church—with practical wisdom, honest confessions, and decades of experience.

Look for these additional parenting resources wherever fine books are sold:

Busy Mom's Guide to Parenting Young Children
Using a question-and-answer format, *Busy Mom's Guide to Parenting Young Children* takes you from birth through age 4 with tips on sleep patterns, potty training, developmental milestones, and more. Tired already? Get energized and equipped for the journey with this quick reference guide, and look forward to the joy of growing with your child.
(Some content previously published in the *Complete Guide to Baby & Child Care*.)

Busy Mom's Guide to Parenting Teens
Using a question-and-answer format, *Busy Mom's Guide to Parenting Teens* gives you tips and solid advice as your child heads into the teen years and develops independence. Driving, cell phones, social networking, physical and emotional changes—your teen is being bombarded with new experiences! Don't just survive your child's leap into adolescence, take the journey together and learn to thrive. Your road map is inside this book—enjoy the ride!
(Some content previously published in the *Complete Guide to Baby & Child Care*.)

Busy Mom's Guide to Family Nutrition
Using a question-and-answer format, *Busy Mom's Guide to Family Nutrition* provides bite-size pieces of information, including nutritional basics, the skinny on fats, interpreting food labels, exploring popular diet plans, and much more. Improve your family's health quotient with this quick reference guide, and enjoy your healthy family!
(Some content previously published in the *Complete Guide to Family Health, Nutrition & Fitness*.)

CP0536